BLISS

A PRACTICAL GUIDE TO TANGO EUPHORIA

Copyright © Aleksey Vays 2025
All Rights Reserved
Cover photos by Iris Rogozhyna

Aleksey Vays has asserted his right to be identified as the author of this Work in accordance with the Copyright, Designs and Patents Act 1988.

No part of this book may be reproduced in any form by photocopying or any electronic or mechanical means including information storage or retrieval systems, without permission in writing from both the copyright owner and publisher of the book.

ISBN13: 979-8-9909827-1-0 (paperback edition)
ISBN13: 979-8-9909827-2-7 (e-book edition)

blissfultango.com
alekseyvays.com
rightontheones.com

DISCLAIMER

The author is not a psychologist, therapist, or medical professional. The contents of this book are based solely on his personal experiences and reflections. They are provided for informational and educational purposes only and are not intended as medical, psychological, or professional advice.

Before attempting any of the exercises or practices described here, consult a qualified healthcare professional — especially if you have any medical or psychological conditions, or if you are unsure whether these activities are appropriate for you.

By reading this book and engaging in any of the described activities, you agree that you do so voluntarily and at your own risk. The author and publisher disclaim any liability for any loss, injury, or damage alleged to arise from the use or misuse of the information contained in this book.

blissfultango.com
alekseyvays.com
rightontheones.com

To the Love of my life,

Fanni

Szeretlek mindennél jobban

Foreword
by Veronica Toumanova (Paris)

One summer day back in 2014, I received an email from a young man who had been dancing tango for five months. He was traveling to Paris and wanted to take some classes. I had been recommended to him by common friends as a good local teacher. He was originally from Ukraine, living in the US at the time, and at the very beginning of his tango journey.

I remember our private class vividly. For a beginner, Aleksey not only had a remarkably mature idea of what he was looking for, but he also had that distinct look that made me chuckle inwardly, "Ah, the tango devil just claimed a new soul." Somewhat brooding in his appearance, saying little but with carefully chosen words, Aleksey was interested in the quality of the embrace and in developing a good walking technique. As a teacher, hearing this from a beginner melts your heart. While I drilled him on his walk, Slavic discipline style, I watched with amusement the serious expression on his face that I recognized so well, one of someone already profoundly lost in tango. Lost as in "you just found something you have been looking for your whole life."

Some fourteen years earlier, I must have had that same look as I plunged headfirst into the mystery of tango. It was a look of someone both obsessed and utterly bewitched. It felt like meeting a "younger brother in tango". We kept in touch over the years. Unsurprisingly, Aleksey became a wonderful dancer quite quickly. But beyond that, he retained the same deep fascination with tango that had drawn him in from the beginning.

Tango seems to tickle analytical minds with a special challenge: a desire to capture its mystery in words. Around the time I met Aleksey, I had begun writing essays about some of the deeper, less surface level aspects of this dance. One day, he told me he wanted to write a book about how to capture and, importantly, recapture when lost, that elusive sensation we call "tango bliss."

Throughout the years, I have had countless conversations, particularly with leaders, about what makes them feel blissful during a dance, why that feeling sometimes disappears, and why it can be so difficult to get it back. For followers it is often easier to bask in bliss because our modus operandi is to trust our intuitive responses to the lead, to melt into the connection and to flow with it. All of which quiets the analytical mind and sets our spontaneous self free to roam. Leaders, unfortunately, do not always have that luxury. I personally believe that this "bliss imbalance" is one of the reasons we see more female followers in tango than male leaders, though not the only reason.

This book is written with honesty and depth from the perspective of a thoughtful and sensitive (straight) male leader. Naturally, certain experiences and insights are colored by Aleksey's personal journey. Yet I find this book just as valuable as a female follower and as an occasional female leader. It offers a wealth of ideas to explore and experiment with in your tango. Some will take you closer to bliss, others may resonate less, but all are worth playing with. With the recent influx of female leaders and the booming Queer Tango community, we may now also be ready for a new understanding of a leader's bliss that is not necessarily rooted in the traditionally gendered roles or heteronormative understanding of masculinity and femininity.

From the start, Aleksey felt like the right person for the task. I thoroughly enjoyed reading this book and I highly recommend it to anyone who wishes to add new and deeper dimensions to their tango experience. I am particularly delighted that someone has taken the time to put into words, and to break down into elements, something so elusive yet so powerful: the bliss of a beautifully connected tanda. Bliss that is accessible, paradoxically, to beginners and professionals alike, or no one would stay in tango beyond their first year, nor continue dancing twenty-five years later. It is the mystery at tango's heart, the feeling we are always seeking, and the reason tango is so hard to explain to those who have never tried it. And we may have just taken another step closer to understanding it.

Table of Contents

Foreword by Veronica Toumanova (Paris) 4
Why I Wrote This Book 11
What Do You *Really* Want? 13
Purpose 17
    Reframe Anxiety as Excitement Exercise 20
Spirals and Waves 22
Controlled Movement 25
    Synchronize Your Step Exercise 27
Breath 27
    Breathe the Music Exercise 30
    Start with the Breath Exercise 31
    Breathe into your Lower Back Exercise 32
Mindfulness 38
    Get into the "Here and Now" Exercise 41
    The Attention Checklist Exercise 42
Attention in Tango Roles 45
Multitasking and the Subconscious Mind 49
    Add a Point to Your "Checklist" Exercise 51
Energy 52
    "Ring of Light" Exercise 53
    Energy Mindset 56
    How Much of Yourself Are You Giving? 59
Emotions 60

Embodying the Music 64
    Embodying the Music with Ecstatic Dance Exercise 65
    Feel the "Off Limits" Emotion of a Tango Composition Exercise 66
    Visualize the Emotions of a Tango Composition Exercise 67

Story 69

Musicality 71

Mapping Music to Movement 72
    Dance Without Taking a Single Step Exercise 77
    Mapping Music to the Push Stage of Your Step 79

Mindful Movement 80
    Excluding One Habitual Movement Exercise 81
    "Musical Chairs" Exercise 82
    Listen for the Accent Dynamics Exercise 83
    Listen for the Volume Dynamics Exercise 84

Pauses 85

Phrases 88
    Walking in a Tight Circle Exercise 89

Simplify 93
    Simplify Your Dance Exercise 94
    Feel the Syncopation Exercise 95
    Step on the "2" and "4" Exercise 95

The 6th Instrument 96

Live Music 97

Abstractions 98
    Focus on the Music Exercise 99

Unspoken Agreements 100

Stability and Technique 101
    Put on Your Shoes while Standing on One Foot Exercise 103

Dissociation Pivots Exercise 105
Our Two Main Spirals 107
Gravity 109
Being Light or Massive 110
    Light or Massive Exercise 112
Improvement 113
Style 119

Psychology 121
Beginner's Journey 123
Know Thyself 124
Mindset 127
Shadow 128
Trauma 133
What if You're Not Getting Invited? 136
A *No* as a Gift 138
Dealing with a Tango Low 142
Your Temple 144
Humor 147

Connection, Communication, and Intimacy 149
    Eye-gazing Exercise 152
The Medium and the Protocol 153
Abstractions 154
Obstacles 157
"Yes!" – an Antidote to Mistakes 158

Partner 160
Choice 163

Invitation 166
Mutual Care and Respect 167
Kindness 168
Embrace 170
   Intention 170
   Qualities 171
   Visualizations and Comparisons 172
   Closeness and Sexuality... 173
   The 3 Types of Embrace 175
   Focus 176
      Inverted Embrace Exercise 177
   The Hand Embrace.. 178
      No Hand Embrace Exercise 178
   The Back Connection 179
   Communication 180
      Stopping the Leader Exercise 181
   The Key to Softness... 181
Compromise 183
Modeling and Mirroring..184
   Coordination Exercise 186

Polarity 187

Oneness 191
Riding the Wave Together..192
Moving as One 193
Dissolving Space and Time 194

Why I Wrote This Book

When Russia began its full-scale invasion and genocide in my home country, I was absolutely devastated. I became as depressed as I've ever been. My mindfulness practices and meditations didn't help. One of my favorite tango marathons, for which I had registered the previous year, was coming up in Budapest.

My first evening of that event was deeply emotional and transformative. I went from the lowest of my lows to the highest of my highs in a matter of minutes. I felt something — so out of my reach for me, and for so long, that I thought it was unattainable. I felt blissful. The change in my state was so profound that it shook me to my core. Then and there I understood viscerally the potential that tango has for me. The realization was clear: not only can tango help me temporarily forget about the horrors, over which I have no control, I can actually experience elation and bliss unlike with any other pastime.

The year is 2023. I'm writing this book as the war continues, though I'm still as optimistic as ever that it will soon end with Ukraine's victory. Several times I have returned home to Kyiv, where I visited all the *milongas*[1] and *practicas*[2] and danced with my favorite partners. Defiant, we continue to dance in the face of ruthless bombing of our cities. "Working on the book at home is the theoretical part,"

---

[1] *milonga* (event) – A social gathering where people dance tango, vals, and milonga (music genre).
[2] A practice event for a group of people to explore and improve tango technique in a relaxed setting.

I tell a wonderful tanguera friend between *tandas*[3], "this — this is my laboratory."

My perspectives are shaped by my personal tango experience as a male *leader*[4], mostly dancing with female *followers*[5]. I wholeheartedly support the notion that tango is for everyone, regardless of their sex, gender, sexual orientation, or choice of role. Most of the ideas in this book are just as valid for female leaders, male followers, and for people who dance both roles, no matter which pronouns are used here. Certain concepts, however, like closeness and sexuality, are not interchangeable between men and women. I believe that a man is responsible for making a woman feel safe, most importantly from himself, regardless of their choice of roles in tango.

I also hope that followers find this book useful and informative, since most of these ideas and exercises apply to them as well. Furthermore, followers may get certain insights into the leader's mind, and this can be invaluable.

I'm writing this book, because I feel that I've discovered a secret — one, to which not so many people are privy. Tango bliss is real, and it's available to anyone, who sets a goal to experience it. Here is a way and methodology to improve your state to whatever degree you want, from "tango helps me forget my problems for a while," all the way to purring-like-a-kitten, hearing-the-angels-sing, cloud-nine euphoria. Whether you're at the beginning or in the middle of your tango journey, or if you're simply looking to identify your possible

---

[3] A set of 3 or 4 songs of the same style played in sequence during a milonga.
[4] The partner who initiates interpretation and direction of movement.
[5] The partner who interprets the lead and responds to the leader's signals.

blind spots, on which you want to work, this book will give you plenty of food for thought.

Throughout this book, you may come across references to geometry, biomechanics, and music theory. If any of this seems too technical or intimidating at first glance, rest assured — it's not. There are no prerequisites for reading this book, and none of it will be on the test. My intention is simply to plant a few seeds of ideas in your mind, which will sprout in their own time.

I want to make this information available and accessible to everyone, no matter their worldview and mindset. My goal is to help as many people as possible to reach a good-feeling place. I love seeing blissed out expressions on people's faces at tango events, and if I can contribute to magnifying their quantity — well, that thought alone makes my heart sing.

What Do You *Really* Want?

There is a subtle, yet profound distinction when it comes to motivation in social tango. We're always looking for pleasure when we dance, but the way we get there is either via intrinsic or extrinsic motivation[6].

Extrinsic motivation has to do with the way your tango looks from the outside. The focus here is on appearance and aesthetics — eye candy. You want your tango to *look* good. Aiming to dance with an

---

[6] https://www.simplypsychology.org/differences-between-extrinsic-and-intrinsic-motivation.html

advanced partner, in order to look particularly sharp on the dance floor is an example of extrinsic motivation. In social dance, extrinsic motivation is also about your status within the community: who are your friends, which partners do you usually dance with, etc.

Intrinsic motivation has to do with the way you *feel* when dancing. Seeking to establish a deep connection with your partner, and to create the kind of magic that can only be experienced directly within the embrace, is an example of intrinsic motivation.

There is no right or wrong here — both of these result in gratification. Your motivation might even change during a milonga, when, after you've danced with the two or three partners on your "list," you switch to drawing pleasure from the wonderful embraces.

With extrinsic motivation, the recommendations are fairly straightforward: to get dances with maestras, and to have your tango look good, you have to practice your technique and take lots of lessons from teachers whose dance you admire.

Intrinsic motivation, on the other hand, is a bit trickier. Your inclination may be to take lessons from teachers, dancing with whom feels particularly pleasurable, and I wholeheartedly support this idea. You can learn a great deal "by osmosis" — by simply dancing with a good teacher, mirroring them, and allowing your body to absorb everything they have to offer. Some concepts of the finer realms, however, are more difficult to learn this way. Perspectives on energy, emotions, intimacy, and psychology, which I want to highlight in this book, leave plenty of room for introspection, reflection, and discussion. These finer realms are the foundation of everything we do on and off the dance floor, and they hold the keys to experiencing reality-altering, perception-bending, time-stopping tango bliss.

You may be one of the lucky tango dancers to whom the state of euphoria on the dance floor comes naturally, and this makes me a bit jealous. The rest of us will "dare to dream" as we set out to understand, practice, and experiment with concepts that will help us get there. If you're a skeptic and think that tango bliss is made up — I assure you, it is absolutely real. This brings us to an important point: your worldview determines your experience. You can only achieve your goals if you believe that they're attainable. Otherwise, time and again, you will sabotage your own actions — even without being aware of this — and fail, proving that you were right in your skepticism. I humbly suggest avoiding that route and simply taking my word for it, at least as a theoretical exercise: you can feel absolute euphoria on the dance floor if you set it as your personal goal.

> *"What a beautiful thought it is to consider that some of the most delightful moments in your life are yet to arrive."*
> —Amber Lyon

Perhaps I'm not the only one who has experienced an evolution of goals during their tango-childhood and tango-adolescence. My cautious venture into tango began when, on the verge of the realization that my wife and I were going to divorce, I was looking for a personal development practice. As soon as tango gave me exactly what I was looking for, my goals changed. Rather, they expanded — it turned out that there are so many wonderful people to meet in social tango! Then, at my first tango festival, I discovered the incredible variety and the sheer quantity of magnificent tango music. Then came traveling to foreign countries and feeling at home as soon as I approached the venue and heard the familiar sounds coming from a place I've never been. My next — and current — goal in tango seems to have eclipsed the previous ones and taken all my time, focus, and attention unto itself: bliss.

This state has many names: from "flow" to being "in the zone," to "riding the wave" to being on a "journey out of time" — across countless practices, and tango is no exception. I began catching glimpses of bliss on the dance floor about five years into my tango life. I found that the feeling of euphoria is often experienced by both partners, and that we're able to take our partner along with us into this state. "Something really nice is starting to happen in your dance," a wonderful tanguera told me when we first danced after a long while of not seeing each other. My unending quest for self-improvement and the countless tango lessons I was taking began to show me that not only is tango bliss real, but we have the potential to experience it systematically. I'm going to dissect and examine the components needed to get there, provide exercises that will help you improve, and create a roadmap to experiencing tango bliss on a regular basis.

Here is my take on the potential elements. It's a pyramid: at the top is the most ethereal and elusive, and at the bottom is the most fundamental and essential.

Oneness
you suspend your personal identity in favor of merging with your partner as one

Polarity
you embody the follower or leader role fully, creating a strong charge between you and your partner

Emotions
you fully immerse yourself in the emotions of the music and embody them

Musicality
your every movement has a purpose, and you embody the energy of the music

Partner
your partner wields the elements below as well as you do, or better

Breath
you are fully in charge of your breath, and your blood is rich with oxygen

Connection, Openness & Authenticity
you're fully open with your partner, and you embody your unique and authentic self

Stability, Axis & Technique
your technique is solid, and you're not relying on your partner to "complete you"

Psychology & Mindset
you're in charge of your thoughts, and you believe that it's possible to experience bliss in tango

Motivation & Purpose
you want to enjoy your dance to the fullest, and you've set it as your goal

In order to experience euphoria when dancing, none of these have to be perfect — even if such a thing were possible. Here I simply want to rank the importance of these ideas and provide you with the opportunity to assess your blind spots. Since you have chosen Argentine tango — a comparatively challenging pastime with a steep learning curve — I'm confident that self-improvement is your thing, and that you will achieve your goals in no time at all.

Purpose

Beyond distinguishing between extrinsic and intrinsic motivation, we can explore a deeper layer: the purpose of your dance. This touches on identity and self-inquiry — how you see yourself and how you see others.

Everything we do, whatever it may be, is ultimately because we *believe* it will make us feel better. This holds true for everyone, regardless of the situation, context, or scale of our goals. Even in the most altruistic or self-sacrificial cases, this principle remains. Our beliefs — especially those we hold about ourselves — shape our motivation before we even think about taking any kind of action.

Tango, as you may have guessed, is no exception. In fact, I would argue that tango vividly illustrates our psychology — from a strictly pragmatic perspective, the act of dancing in and of itself is entirely useless. So what are you really after? What is the purpose of your dance in this moment? Broadly speaking, there are two opposing categories of purpose in dance: self-expression and self-validation.

Self-validation is the fleeting satisfaction of a desire for a label or approval, which usually comes from the outside — from someone else. Even when I label or evaluate myself, it is still self-validation by definition.

Self-expression, on the other hand, is a state where no labels or evaluations are needed. It arises when my sense of who I am comes from within and is reflected in my thoughts, words, and actions.

My dance reflects my objective. If I'm dancing to validate myself, I'm pursuing a valuation — from myself or from others. Does my partner like dancing with me? How can I make a good impression? What do others think of me? I begin comparing myself to other dancers. My inner dialogue turns into an argument between a "good cop" and a "bad cop," consuming most of my attention and putting my movements on autopilot. Dance becomes secondary. Comparisons and judgments also bring discomfort, no matter who ends up on the losing side.

If I'm dancing to express myself, I am guided only by what's inside, focused on my state. This integrity frees me from the need for valuations or comparisons. Liberation, as a result, manifests in my dance. By liberating myself, I also set an example for others. What am I feeling in this moment? What is my partner feeling? There is no inner dialogue — I'm here and now.

You can probably guess which of these purposes leads to bliss and which takes you away from it. And I can already hear the objections: "Easy for you to say!"

A dear friend once told me about an interesting phenomenon she noticed at El Corte milongas in the Netherlands: "The dance hall at this milonga is dimly lit and separated from the *cabeceo*[7] lounge by a corridor. From the entrance, you can only see part of the dance floor — the near side of the *ronda*[8]. I dance with my eyes closed, and I could distinctly feel when we passed in front of the 'display.' In that moment, my partner's dance tangibly changed, even if only for a brief time." If a separated dance floor is unusual, then what about all the other milongas, where dancers are visible all the time?

What can you do if you feel anxious or experience "stage fright" when people watch you dance? Doesn't it push you into a headspace of valuation, comparison, and judgment? From quantum physics we know that the very act of observation changes what is observed. The first step is to accept this as a fact — just as inevitable as people watching the dancers at a milonga.

---

[7] Traditional method of inviting someone to dance using a subtle head nod after a *mirada*.
[8] The organized flow of dancing couples around the dance floor in a counter-clockwise direction.

Second, we can borrow a technique from psychology. Studies suggest that we can reframe our perception of anxiety as excitement. Since both anxiety and excitement are high-arousal states, it is easier to shift from anxiety to excitement than from anxiety to calm. When we reframe anxiety as excitement, we remain in a high-arousal state and shift from a threat mindset to an opportunity mindset. What's most fascinating is that simply saying the phrase "I'm excited" is often enough to make the switch.

> **REFRAME ANXIETY AS EXCITEMENT EXERCISE**
>
> Next time you feel social anxiety rising before a tanda, take charge by taking a deep inhale and exhale. Say the phrase "I'm excited!" out loud. Don't fight the state your body is adopting — lean into it instead. Use that high-arousal state to your advantage. Remember, there's no threat here, only wonderful opportunities. When your partner asks how you're doing, reply with something like: "I'm excited — this is such a wonderful event! The music is amazing! I've been looking forward to this!"

Third, you can actually use the energy of onlookers in your dance. At milongas, I try to feel the whole room — the entire space, along with everyone present. When I inhale, I imagine inhaling the energy of the room, regardless of the quality of its individual constituents. The reason the quality doesn't matter is that human beings are energy alchemists. With clear intention, we can transmute energy into whatever quality we choose. I consciously turn the energy of the room into joy and allow it to flow through my dance.

Experienced performers excel at this kind of alchemy. Have you noticed how a truly great performance feels a thousand times more powerful live than it does in a recording? That's because the audience, through real-time observation, becomes part of the performance. By focusing on the dancers, the audience amplifies the couple's energy. This creates a powerful resonance between the couple in the spotlight and everyone watching. Skilled performers "breathe the room" and transform that amplified energy into a mesmerizing experience for everyone present.

The fourth point is quite simple: most people are too preoccupied with themselves to even notice you. They may appear to be watching the dancers, but their minds are usually elsewhere. So you can relax — no one is really paying that much attention.

But what if you hesitate to fully express yourself in dance because you're afraid that unkind or unattractive parts of your personality might surface? Many people avoid looking inward for fear of discovering uncomfortable aspects of their character. Perhaps you've caught glimpses of these parts before and decided to hide them away, making sure no one ever sees them. Problem solved, right?

Unfortunately, this approach doesn't just block fulfillment in your dance — it also limits satisfaction in your professional and personal life. Fear creates inner resistance — a constant background tension that drains your energy, adds stress, and undermines your health. I suspect part of the reason tango dancers enjoy festivals and marathons so much is that dancing around the clock for several days physically exhausts them to the point where they simply don't have the resources to maintain their usual inner resistance. It's a roundabout way to find a bit of peace. So what's the alternative?

The path to truly enjoying your experience — whether in dance or in life — leads through healing. Without it, the unhealed parts of your psyche will always get in the way of your bliss. We will dive deeper into this subject in *Psychology*.

Spirals and Waves

"Pleasure may be found by absorbing ourselves in questions of pure geometry."
—Albert Einstein

Science is coming closer to understanding that spin is an inherent property of spacetime[9]. When we add progression to spin, we get a movement trajectory in the shape of a three-dimensional helix. Most of nature's movements are in the shape of a spiral, including the propagation of sound, light, and the motion of our planet and the solar system as they move through the Milky Way. Our galaxy, as you can imagine, isn't fixed in place, either, but the general idea is clear. The muscles in the heart contract in a specific sequence, spinning our blood as it's pumped through the arteries. The air spirals as it travels through our nasal passages. The muscle groups, tendons, and fascia are naturally arranged as spirals around our torso and limbs, creating a fractal spiral in our body. The examples are countless.

---

[9] Haramein, N. & Rauscher, E. A. THE ORIGIN OF SPIN: A CONSIDERATION OF TORQUE AND CORIOLIS FORCES IN EINSTEIN'S FIELD EQUATIONS AND GRAND UNIFICATION THEORY (2004).

Spiral dynamics create the most natural movement[10]. Spiral dynamics in the movements of our partner feel divine in the dance. If you're inclined to equate nature's genius with beauty, then you will also find spiral dynamics beautiful to observe in dancers. We can examine spirals as trajectories of movement with various geometric properties.

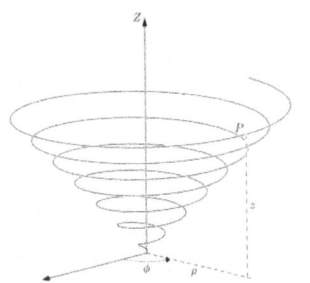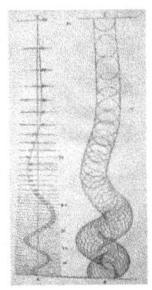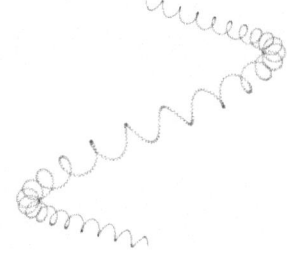

In the image above, the spiral on the left opens — its radius increases — with distance from the origin (at the origin this spiral appears closed). The spiral in the middle demonstrates a different dynamic — the distance between its turns increases with height. This spiral unwinds toward the top and winds toward the bottom. This spiral appears closed at both ends. The spiral on the right is an example of a different type of complexity — a nested helix — a smaller spiral wound in the shape of a larger spiral. This image shows a fractal with three distinct levels of self-similarity: tiny turns wound into medium turns, wound into a large turn. This particular spiral appears open in both directions.

When you consider the number of possibilities created by combinations of these analog properties in spirals, you will quickly realize

---

[10] Larsen, C. (2019). Spiraldynamik®: Becoming and remaining pain-free and flexible. Zürich, Switzerland: Spiraldynamik Institut.

that the number is infinite. Each trajectory of movement, each spiral, each dance, is unique.

In tango figures, spirals show up in various ways. Each time you *dissociate*[11], you're embodying a helix. When a *giro*[12] ends with a *parada*[13], the follower's right foot draws a closing spiral. In a *milonguero dip*[14], both partners share a closing spiral. Opening the embrace during a *calesita*[15] opens the leader's spiral around the follower. The examples are many.

We also find that much of the propagation, interaction, and movement in nature occurs in waves. From the propagation of sound through a medium to the explosions of supernovae, waves are a universal phenomenon. Nature rarely moves in blocks; in order to see the wave, one may simply need to adjust the frame of reference. When the concept of waves is applied to the human body, it translates into the sequence and timing of movements. When you consider the stages of an *enrosque*[16], for example, you will see that it's comprised of waves. These waves begin in the leader's upper body (winding the spiral) and travel downward (unwinding the spiral).

---

[11] Rotate the upper body independently from the hips.
[12] A circular turn, typically led around the leader's axis.
[13] A brief, intentional stop where the leader halts the follower's movement by gently placing a foot in front of the follower.
[14] A figure, which involves a circular, counterclockwise downward closing of a spiral, resulting in the follower's pivot.
[15] Carousel-like movement where one partner pivots while the other circles around them.
[16] A turning figure where the leader pivots on one leg while drawing the other leg around it in a spiral, creating a controlled rotation.

"In the wave lies the secret of creation."
—Walter Russell

Spirals and helixes mainly describe the 3-dimensional geometry of natural movement; waves point to its 4th dimension, which is time. You will see that this dimension is a treasure chest of its own when you consider various possible types of acceleration and deceleration. Dance and body movement can uncover a path to a very special kind of bliss by slowing down time itself.

Controlled Movement

By definition, every controlled movement has a smaller force vector aimed in the opposite direction. This subtle counterforce usually initiates and prepares the movement. To demonstrate this, simply ask someone to jump up. The very first thing they do is crouch down to prepare for the jump. In dance, our movements are usually much more subtle than jumps, and this counterforce rarely appears as visible movement, but it is always present.

The counterforce is easier to feel than to see. You'll notice it if you pay attention to the initial stages of a tango step. For example, the forward step begins with a "backward" opening spiral. It originates from stillness — or from ongoing motion, if the

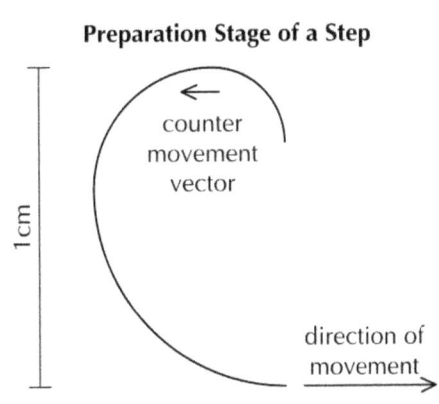

Preparation Stage of a Step

body is already moving — and unfolds upward, backward, then downward and forward. To get a sense of just how subtle this backward loop is, you can think of its diameter as being no more than a centimeter. This backward direction is the counterforce vector expressed at the very start of a controlled forward step.

Throughout the step, the counterforce vector continues to manifest as a subtle energy aimed opposite to the direction of movement. A pertinent question here would be, "Why exert extra effort by adding a force vector, which you know will be negated?" It is precisely because this counterforce makes the movement *controlled*. For example, the size and direction of a controlled step can be adjusted at any point. The step can be stopped short or even reversed. All these possibilities are invaluable when communicating with a partner or navigating a crowded ronda.

This counterforce vector adds a new dimension to our interaction in the dance. It makes movement feel spacious and three-dimensional. When a follower engages a "high setting" for her counterforce vector, dancing with her can feel like moving through honey. A simple tango walk becomes a source of immense pleasure when both partners are "walking through honey" together. When a leader engages his counterforce vector, he invites the follower to do the same and communicates stability and control.

Although the counterforce vector is present during the entire movement, it is most pronounced in the preparation stage. This allows us to use it as a form of communication within the couple and to synchronize our movements.

> **SYNCHRONIZE YOUR STEP EXERCISE**
>
> Practice this with your partner in tango embrace, with or without music. Keep in mind that your pelvis is your body's powerhouse, and your pushing leg does all the work. In preparation for a step, leaders can imagine and embody the following: move your center in a small backward "loop" — up, back, down, and only then forward, taking a step together with your partner. This loop's diameter is subtle, only about a centimeter. Followers, tune in to the leaders and pay close attention to this preparatory stage. Its subtlety may call for extra sensitivity.
>
> The preparatory stage of side steps and back steps (for leaders) follows the same dynamic. For instance, the preparatory loop for a step to the right goes up, left, down, and then right.

The magic of synchronized movement creates the feeling and appearance of the tango couple moving as one entity and brings us closer to bliss on the dance floor.

Breath

"Don't forget to breathe!" Suddenly everyone in the group lesson remembered that we all have lungs. What's interesting is that before the teacher's remark, we were all breathing, just differently. Then everyone took a deep inhale and exhale, and for a few seconds the exercise became easier.

Breath is the only function of the body that can be both conscious and unconscious. Yogis and Buddhists suggest conscious breathing as a "way to yourself," a connection with the spirit. I cannot promise that you will reach enlightenment by focusing on your breath, but I can guarantee that tango bliss is out of the question if your breath is on autopilot. When we breathe unconsciously, it often becomes shallow, which has many negative effects on health — let alone the state of euphoria we're after. For tango bliss, the essentials are feeling well and having oxygen-rich blood.

Some time ago I discovered that in any situation, taking a conscious inhale and exhale immediately helps me in several ways. Instead of reacting, I'm able to respond to outside factors. It helps me focus in the present moment, take control of my psychological state, and take charge of my volition. The last one is critical when dancing because volition — being in the driver's seat and choosing my actions — is the origin of authenticity in tango.

In many situations, circumstances can pull us away from volition and make it seem as if outside factors are determining our experience. Social tango, as a miniature model of life, presents plenty of these situations. To remind myself that I'm in charge of my own experience, all I need to do is take a conscious inhale and exhale.

In tango, there are several realms of connection: with ourselves, with the music, with the floor, with our partner, and with the other couples on the dance floor. Our breath, together with body awareness and perception of sensory information, is a central part of our connection with ourselves. I believe breath is also the bridge between our connection with ourselves and our connection with the music.

If we contemplate the ethereal nature of music, and the fact that we perceive audio waves as they travel through air, we begin to sense how much similarity there is between our breath and music. The singing you hear in lyrical tango compositions is the vocalist's breath turned into a musical instrument. This is awe-inspiring. The bandoneon, a wind instrument, also has its own inhales and exhales. There are many such parallels. If we consider conscious breathing as our connection with ourselves, it allows us to express ourselves more clearly and freely in the dance, and enhances our musicality and improvisation.

If you listen to any tango composition, you will notice a rhythm of a different kind — its breath rhythm, the way you might want to breathe while dancing to it. For example, your breath rhythm may align with the musical phrases, where each inhale-exhale corresponds to one phrase, though this is not a rule. Understandably, this is subjective, and no composition has a single "correct" breath rhythm. Your breathing will be unique, shaped by many factors during the dance. The most important thing is to consciously "listen" to the music with your breath.

When should you inhale, and when should you exhale? Tango music often has a clear dynamic of swells and troughs — rising and falling levels of energy. Many elements contribute to this: volume, tonality, tempo changes, emotional expression, and dominant instruments. Yet these shifts in energy are usually easier to feel than to analyze. In general, I tend to inhale when the energy rises and exhale when it falls.

But don't stress over the details. Don't hold your breath during a long pause in the music, and don't mimic *staccato*[17] by breathing in bursts. Forgive lapses, generalize, and keep things simple. Most importantly, remember to "breathe the music." Your musicality will reflect it, and your improvisation will come easily and naturally.

> **BREATHE THE MUSIC EXERCISE**
>
> a) Pick a romantic composition (e.g. *Mi Tango Triste* - Anibal Troilo with Alberto Marino) and breathe it by yourself, without dancing. You'll begin to notice your own interpretation of the composition's breath rhythm.
> b) Pick a tango composition and breathe it while walking alone. Since movement requires a bit more oxygen, this version of the exercise more closely reflects the conditions in which you'll find your natural breath rhythm.
> c) Pick a lyrical composition and breathe it while standing still in a close embrace with your partner. Feeling your partner's swells and troughs — and allowing them to feel yours — can help you connect on a deeper level. You may discover your partner's unique interpretation of the composition's breath rhythm and realize that there can be a dance without steps, a dance in the breath itself. When you and your partner tune in to each other, try synchronizing your breath. Then experiment with the opposite: inhale when your partner exhales, and vice versa. Who is leading, and who is following? There's plenty of room for play here.

---

[17] A style of playing music in which the notes are short and clearly separated from one another.

> d) Pick a composition and breathe it while walking in a close embrace with your partner. A slower, lyrical composition may be especially helpful for identifying its breath rhythm. This version of the exercise will bring you closer to truly breathing the music on the dance floor.

If you're finding it difficult to add conscious breathing to your multitasking stack, try incorporating it one step at a time. Begin a composition with your breath. In other words, breathe the music as the starting point for movement. This can serve as a helpful stepping stone.

> **START WITH THE BREATH EXERCISE**
>
> Add breath to your attention checklist. When you embrace your partner at the beginning of a tanda, resist the urge to move right away. Take a few seconds to connect, and take a conscious inhale and exhale, gently inviting your partner to join you. Make this a habit and do it at the start of every tanda you dance.

Note that your breathing and your partner's do not have to synchronize; what matters is bringing conscious breathing into your dance.

Start noticing the way you breathe off the dance floor as well: when talking with your partner, walking, working, or making love. Compare a deep breath you take after a long, tiring day with one you take while enjoying fresh air out in nature. How quickly do you inhale? Is your breath choppy, wavy, or smooth? Does it accelerate or slow down? The qualities of your breath reflect both your physiological and emotional state. And in close embrace, your partner will have the chance to sense it all.

What's a good way to breathe? I suggest breathing through your nose, since that is its primary function. As for where to direct your inhale, you have several options. Try experimenting with the following approaches to see what feels best for you.

When you're asleep, you usually breathe into your belly. Expanding your ribcage when you inhale puts unnecessary pressure on your heart, so you may want to avoid that. Yogis suggest breathing into your lower back, all the way down into your kidneys, so that your belly button actually moves slightly toward your spine when you inhale. Yes, that's correct. When you breathe this way, your back expands and rounds out slightly — and if you recall what your tango teachers have been saying, this is also good for your embrace. It's a double win.

> **BREATHE INTO YOUR LOWER BACK EXERCISE**
>
> Stand up straight. Breathe through your nose, slowing and deepening each breath. Direct your inhalations into your lower back — imagine the air reaching down toward your kidneys. Allow your entire back to expand to accommodate each inhale. Take care not to bend forward or slouch as your back expands. The expansion should be more horizontal than vertical, and it shouldn't affect your posture.

Indeed, a great deal of communication in tango takes place in the contact between your back and your partner's hand. Wouldn't you want to downplay or hide your breathing from your partner? No — breath is another subtle form of communication. Tango, although similar in some ways, is not martial arts, where you might want to hide your breathing to conceal your next move. In tango, we want to be as open as possible with our partner, so it's a good idea to communicate through breath as well. All it takes is being comfortable breathing the music while in your partner's embrace — and also being comfortable with your partner's breathing.

Should your breath be noisy? Not at all. Yogis suggest that your nasal passages remain open and free. If needed, moderate your breath in the trachea instead.

How exactly is breathing a mode of communication? Breath is the starting point of movement. I would even say that it slightly *precedes* movement. In sports, yoga, martial arts, and dance, students inevitably arrive at this axiom. Breath also suggests the *type* of movement. Yogis claim that every pose has a unique breath pattern, though there are some general tendencies. Inhaling suggests going up, expanding, and opening the spiral. Exhaling suggests going down, contracting, and closing the spiral. Inhaling is drawing energy in; exhaling is releasing it.

If you pay attention to your breath, you'll see that this rings true on an intuitive level. In other words, to use breathing as an extra layer of communication, you don't need to learn anything new — simply tune in to your partner. When you're tuned in on the dance floor, and you sense your partner finishing an *inhale* as the phrase is ending, you already have a good idea of what will come next, even before the lead. That is magic!

Tango compositions are full of delightful moments that beg to be expressed through breath. Take *Romance de Barrio* – Anibal Troilo with Floreal Ruiz, for example. This piece has several micro-pauses or slow-downs where, if you *inhale* leading up to them, you create a suspended, weightless feeling, which can only be described as zero-gravity bliss. The music rises, opens, slows, and pauses for just a fraction of a second before reversing back down. If your breath and spirals follow this dynamic, you'll generate a buoyant, ethereal sensation for both you and your partner. It feels as if your breath stops time itself — the moment of weightlessness at the apex becomes a micro eternity. Sure, you exhale as you reverse and unwind your spiral with the music right afterward, but that wonderful feeling stays with both of you.

There are also moments in tango music where the energy dissipates. This usually happens at the end of a key phrase, when a somber mood brings the energy down to the point where it ceases to exist. Instead of movement, these mournful passages ask for nothing more than a simple *exhale*.

Taking charge of your breath can also help when dealing with fast music. Conscious breathing has the power to alter our perception of time. If you want more time to hit those sixteenth notes, try slowing down and deepening your breath. Of course, the music won't change, but your focus will sharpen, and your level of concentration will rise to meet the challenge.

Breathing consciously immerses you in the present moment. Suddenly, there's no airtime for distracting thoughts, and this is what allows you to "slow down time". Your movements become easier and more precise. With oxygen-rich blood, your body feels lighter and more responsive.

By a similar principle, voluntary breathing heightens sensitivity[18]. Your peripheral nervous system is responsible for sensory perception — how your body perceives the outside world. When oxygen-rich blood reaches your brain and nervous system, it expands the range of perception, increasing the amount of information you can take in through your senses. Put simply, breathing well enhances your ability to feel.

Shallow[19] or rapid breathing may be a sign that a person is not fully present. They may be thinking about yesterday, worrying about what others think, or focusing anywhere but the dance, the "here and now." Of course, there are many possible reasons for shallow breathing: psychological blockages, trauma, or cultural conditioning, to name just a few. When we repress our feelings, which is the common denominator in this list, it tends to restrict our breath.

Another reason tango dancers may avoid breathing fully is the fear it could be misinterpreted as lust or sexual overtones. Yet in the embrace, breathing the music and breathing lustfully are very different — the qualities and emotions of the breath are worlds apart. If your height difference puts your nose near your partner's ear, you can simply turn your head slightly to avoid breathing directly into it.

My main suggestion is to trust that your partner will not misinterpret your breathing. Sure, tango is a play between the masculine and the feminine components present in all of us, and often the polarized charge between partners can be very strong. But the difference between this play and luring someone sexually is clear: tango un-

---

[18] https://jonlieffmd.com/blog/breathing-alters-perception
[19] https://blog.calm.com/blog/shallow-breathing

folds here and now, on the dance floor. Luring, by contrast, is a fantasy projected into the future; the one projecting is not fully present, and that energy is entirely different from dancing polarity in the moment. If someone chooses to misinterpret your breathing, allow the mistake to be on their side. Don't let a social fear lead you to compromise your breath when dancing.

I remember being particularly astounded in an advanced tango class in Buenos Aires. Our teachers showed us how to lead a *voleo*[20] by dropping the energy and exhaling at the same time. To my surprise, it actually began to work toward the end of the lesson, once we started paying attention to our partners' subtle energy changes. "If I lead this with a hundred partners, maybe two of them will follow it," I told the teacher. She replied, "We don't teach you how to dance with everyone. We teach you how to dance well."

When tango teachers talk about the upward vector of your axis, they often suggest "thinking up." This, however, can feel a bit abstract as a visualization. Instead, consider "breathing up." Breathing already implies movement, so it may be easier to guide this subtle motion with conscious awareness. By "breathing up," I mean visualizing your inhale as a beam of light rising from your spine into the space above your head. The higher it goes, the better. As a result, the natural motion of your breath will make the subtle but necessary adjustments in your axis.

Many tango students focus mainly on the downward vector of their axis, which sends their center of gravity down and provides stability. Of course, this vector is important. But if you focus on it too much, this may have unwanted consequences: your attention and gaze

---

[20] A whipping leg motion, typically executed as a response to a lead during turns.

may drop, your head may tilt forward, and you may feel "heavy to dance with." Breathing up can help you align your upward vector and avoid these issues entirely — while still maintaining stability and a low center of gravity.

When I began "breathing up" on the dance floor, I discovered another bonus — it helped regulate my body temperature. I can't say exactly how this shift in breathing and posture improved heat radiation; all I know is that breathing up helps me stay a bit cooler while dancing. When I dance several tandas in a row, I tend to overheat, so I'm always looking for ways to cool down.

Yoga teaches another method of cooling through breath: inhale through a small opening in your mouth so the air brushes against the top surface of your tongue. Dogs naturally do an exaggerated version of this to regulate temperature, though in yoga you exhale through the nose. The physics behind it is simple: when water evaporates from a surface, it cools both the surface and the air.

The quality of the air we breathe matters a great deal. You can often recognize experienced organizers by how much attention they give to airing out the space and keeping the air fresh and at a comfortable temperature. Personal hygiene is also a big part of this, as well as avoiding the smell of cigarettes or strong perfume. In other words, it's always a good idea to let your partner breathe clean air. I happen to be hypersensitive to smells, and unfortunately this sometimes creates problems for me on the dance floor. At times, my partner's perfume irritates me so much that — forget bliss — I'm trying to survive until the end of this tanda.

There's a lot to your breath in tango. My main suggestion is to approach breath as an integral part of your dance, to see your breath as the dance itself. Let your movement become secondary, a natural continuation of your breath. Your body will quickly reward you with happiness hormones, which are essential to experiencing bliss on the dance floor.

Mindfulness

When I was in my early twenties, I was experiencing periodic depressions. Antidepressant drugs proved to be a failed experiment for me, I was still on the lookout for a solution. Then one day Anastasia, a dear friend of mine, came to our band rehearsal, and handed me a book[21]. "Here," she said, "this is the good stuff." The book described the nature of our thoughts as being quite different from what I used to believe. Our thoughts, the author claimed, are not part of us. They're not even *ours*. Thoughts are like clouds in the sky, or radio waves — we can choose to focus on one, or just as easily switch our focus to another. This choice in the context of thoughts began to reveal to me the true nature of freedom.

This new understanding dramatically changed my relationship with thoughts. Before, when a negative thought appeared in my mind, I used to focus on it without realizing that I have a choice in the matter, and the thought would take me into a downward spiral toward a personalized inferno. With this new understanding, when a negative thought appeared in my mind, I would simply smile and focus

---

[21] Zhikarentsev, V. Put' k svobode: Karmicheskie prichiny vozniknoveniya problem, ili kak izmenit' svoyu zhizn' [The Path to Freedom: Karmic Causes of Problems, or How to Change Your Life]. Ves' Mir, 1998.

on something else. My depressions stopped entirely. This marked the beginning of a life-long self-improvement journey. Even more, following this book's advice showed me a glimpse of the potential that's available to each one of us — the potential to consciously change my psychological state, and to change my experience as a result. My psychology, it turned out, is quite malleable.

If you pay attention, you will see that modern culture is inundated with competition. Aside from sport, people compete in business, at work and in school. Even family bonds sometimes exhibit rivalry. It's no wonder many people approach Argentine tango with a competitive mindset. It would be fine if Mundial and tango championships would be the extent of it, but, unfortunately, competitiveness has found its way into social tango as well. In the context of intrinsic motivation and for the purposes of this book, competitive mentality will only get in the way.

There are other motivators, which get in the way of you experiencing bliss on the dance floor. You may even be unaware that you're driven by some of them. One such example is if you want everyone to love dancing with you. In most cases, the real mechanism behind these counterproductive motivators is your ego chasing its own tail. The main idea is that you don't want your psychology to be an obstacle to what you're really after — to your experiencing euphoria. This is the real effort: to notice, to work on, and to dissolve your own psychological obstacles, which used to get in the way. The result of the dissolution of whatever used to obstruct or limit you, will feel divine.

It's a good idea to know the real reason why you're going to dance this particular tanda with this particular partner right now. There can even be several reasons, but one of them will be key. Your reasons can come from the heart — self-expression, or they can come from your ego — self-validation. Your reasons can be oriented more toward your partner — "I want my partner to feel good," or they can be oriented more toward yourself — "I want to feel good." Your reasons can even be pragmatic — "I need to warm up," or "I'm new here, so I'll invite this brilliant partner, in order for people to see me on the dance floor and want to dance with me."

Whatever is your main reason, be honest with yourself about it. The chances of you hitting the target are higher if you know what your target is. Also, you will not harbor any illusions about hitting all of the targets with one shot.

In order to enjoy your dance to the fullest, all your attention must be focused entirely on the dance itself. Your attention must be focused on your breath, on your partner, on the music, on the traffic, and on your choice of movement — on all that, which comprises the "here and now" on the dance floor.

Focusing all your attention on one thing, however, may not be as easy as it sounds. The content and direction of thoughts, similar to our breath, can be voluntary or involuntary. The involuntary mind is on autopilot; each consecutive thought appears to lead the mind in whatever direction the thought is oriented. In this scenario the thoughts are in charge of the mind. This may seem like quite an inversion, but this is the reality for most people, most of the time. The voluntary mind, on the other hand, is in the driver's seat — there's a clear presence of choice and, thus, control of its content and heading. The voluntary mode means you're fully in charge of the direction of your thoughts. Your focused attention, in this case, is truly your choice.

How do you switch to the voluntary mode? First, you need to set an intention. Like many aspects of human nature, the mode of your mind is shaped by habit. If the involuntary mode feels more comfortable, it's because you've spent more time there. It may also be because the involuntary mode is easier — the genius of our bodies naturally optimizes and redistributes resources as needed.

Your mind, much like a muscle, has to be exercised regularly if you want results. The voluntary mode takes a bit more energy, but it's well worth it. Shifting your mind into this mode, and keeping it there, may take practice. However, once you begin to notice results, that will be all the motivation you need. And not only will your tango benefit — your mood, your health, and your relationships may improve as well.

Like our breath, the mind's voluntary mode is about volition. It's about reclaiming freedom by remembering that we always have a choice, no matter the situation. And we can always return to the breath to turn this understanding into a practical anchor.

GET INTO THE "HERE AND NOW" EXERCISE

Take one voluntary inhale and exhale through the nose, slightly longer and deeper than your usual breath. Set an intention to do this whenever you notice your mind slipping into autopilot. This anchor will immediately help you switch to the voluntary mode and bring you into the "here and now." Set an intention to take a voluntary inhale and exhale whenever you face an unpleasant situation and feel that you're about to react. This anchor will help you transform your reactions into responses.

One practice that helped me center and focus during my tango adolescence was the "attention checklist." This simple yet effective tool helped me integrate and embody everything my teachers had taught me. At different stages of my learning, some of the items on the checklist changed, but the practice itself remained — and proved very useful. Moving the focus of your attention through your body is also a wonderful way to center yourself and become present.

It's not necessary to *always* keep your checklist in mind while dancing. It's enough to simply begin with it. By doing so, you give instructions to your subconscious and allow your body to make the adjustments in its own time. Your body is wiser than you may believe. Think of this ritual as listing tasks and delegating them to your body, without the need to micromanage.

Below is my checklist from some time ago. Its order allowed me to scan my body from the top down:

-Breath
-Ears up
-Eyes forward
-Embracing my partner with my "wings"
-Soft chest
-No tension in my left hand
-My legs begin around my solar plexus
-Center of gravity down
-Engaged feet

THE ATTENTION CHECKLIST EXERCISE

At the start of every tanda, as you embrace your partner, mentally go through your "attention checklist." In your mind's eye, scan your

> body from your head down to your feet. Move slowly enough to notice each item and make small adjustments. Include everything you're working on, such as breath, mindset, gaze, posture, engagement, orientation, and anything else that's on your personal list.

The brain is fascinating. It constantly optimizes and prioritizes tasks in the background, often without our conscious involvement. Movements we repeat many times tend to become automatic — why spend extra energy on something we already know how to do? How often do you notice that, whatever you've been doing for the last several minutes, you've been doing it "on autopilot" while your thoughts drifted somewhere else entirely?

When we perform mundane, familiar tasks like walking home or washing the dishes, our movements seem to happen on their own, without conscious direction. A small part of the mind carries out these habitual motions, while most of it is busy with unrelated thoughts.

On the one hand, walking home or washing the dishes may seem harmless to put on autopilot. On the other hand, mindfulness practices encourage us to be fully present as often as possible, no matter how boring the task may seem. And if you're looking for bliss on the dance floor, autopilot mode is your enemy. Dance is, above all, presence — and autopilot is its polar opposite.

So how do you avoid slipping into autopilot mode? Practice mindfulness on the dance floor. One way is to challenge yourself by dancing to tango music you've never heard before, or at least to music you don't know by heart. This will push you to truly listen. You can also dance with a beginner, which is an excellent way to tune in to your partner. What matters most is your willingness to expend a little extra mental energy and your determination to give your full attention to the dance.

It goes without saying that carrying a conversation while dancing at a milonga is a bad idea. As my driver's education teacher once said, "If you're making love while driving a car, you're doing both things equally poorly." There are other activities on this side of the awareness spectrum that people sometimes mix with dancing. Chewing gum is one. Checking whether your friends have arrived, or looking for your next potential partner on the dance floor, are others. My recommendation regarding all of these is simple: don't do it.

But what if the annoyance is outside your control? What if the couple behind you in the ronda is talking? What if the dance floor traffic is unbearable? Take a voluntary inhale and exhale to regain charge of your psychology, and choose what you want to focus on. This may feel challenging at first, but with practice you'll be able to focus so deeply on the dance that you no longer notice the annoyances. Of course, the talking couple will still be there, but you won't give them any of your mental airtime. If you treat tango as a form of meditative practice, you may even come to see annoyances as opportunities to train and strengthen your focus.

You have far more control over your psychological state than you might believe. It may seem as though outside factors have the power to change how you feel in the moment, when in fact it is your reaction to those factors that causes the change. Once you begin to notice that you have a choice, your reactions can turn into responses. And when you recognize that every moment is one of those moments, you take charge of your own psyche. All that's required to shift into the psychological state of your choice is your intention and your trust that it's possible.

Of course, certain actions can help, and dancing is definitely one of them. Imagine you're in a bad mood after a long day at work, debating whether you even want to go to a milonga in such a state. You decide to go, trusting that your mood will improve. Your intention and your trust are already present; dancing then becomes the catalyst that brings about the change you want.

Noticing the presence of choice — and actively choosing your thoughts, your psychological state, and your actions — is the essence of freedom. Free from endless thoughts, free from old patterns of behavior, and free from the direct pull of outside factors, you return to your authentic self. In this way, dance, as pure artistic self-expression, becomes the embodiment of freedom. It is this process that brings you the state of bliss as a reward. The euphoria you feel is your body's way of expressing gratitude for setting yourself free.

Attention in Tango Roles

Have you ever wondered why leading and following feel so different from each other? I've been leading since the beginning of my tango life, and it's never been intuitive for me to simply switch to following. It's not that I don't know the technique or the figures from the follower's repertoire — I do. What makes switching roles difficult is the way my mind has been trained to *use attention* while dancing.

Attention is a deliberate projection of our consciousness. It can be focused on one spot, or it can be expanded, spread around the periphery. Leading and following rely on these two distinct modes. The leader must first focus inward to tune in to the signal. Leading requires focused attention to then project information and communicate intent to the follower. For example, when leading a step, the leader chooses a point in space — such as a spot on the floor — where the follower's foot should land. The leader focuses attention on that point, and the body, through stretching and contracting muscles, builds up and releases its spirals, thus communicating the information to the follower.

Conversely, in order to tune in to the signal, the follower has to focus outward. Following requires attention that is more spread out, tuned to receiving information. This openness makes it possible to sense what the leader is communicating and to respond immediately in a reflective way.

Scientists distinguish between two modes of thinking: fast and slow[22]. Slow thinking is what most people usually mean when they talk about "thinking" in the classical sense. It's the process of taking in various inputs, running a kind of mental computation, and then producing a result. For instance, this is the mode your brain uses when asked to multiply 12 by 19. Slow thinking requires focused attention, and we access it when we project our consciousness in a focused way.

Fast thinking, on the other hand, is more intuitive and reactive. As the name suggests, it usually takes less time than its slower counterpart. For example, you'll likely use fast thinking if asked to pick out

---

[22] Kahneman, D. Thinking, Fast and Slow. Farrar, Straus and Giroux, 2011.

the tallest person in a group. We engage this mode when our attention is projected peripherally.

Leading, which depends on focused attention, relies more on analytical, slow thinking. A leader has to take in several inputs: the traffic (hopefully), the available 3D space, the time a movement will take, the partner and their skill level, and of course, the music. The leader then processes all of this and, as a result, moves in a way that communicates the lead.

Following, on the other hand, draws more on the reactive, intuitive brain. It engages fast thinking, which produces a continuous flow of immediate, reflective responses to the lead.

Tango teachers often tell followers to "stop thinking!" It's not that they want you to lower your IQ — they want you to shift from the analytical to the intuitive mindset. The goal is for you to move by reflecting the signal you receive from the leader. If you try to analyze the lead, your movement will come too late — we're already on the next bar. That's why a follower's attention should be deliberately distributed around the periphery, simultaneously encompassing the variables. Fortunately for followers there are only two: the partner and the music. This allows you to take in the entire input at once and immediately transform it into movement.

This difference in how we use attention when leading and following creates an imbalance: tango bliss is more readily accessible to followers than to leaders. The state of trance is closer to the expanded projection of consciousness — similar to meditation — than it is to focused attention and computation, which are more like brainwork. The latter tends to pull us away from bliss. This may help explain why more followers stay in tango — their path to euphoria is relatively straightforward, while leaders sometimes struggle to find their way into the zone.

The more advanced a follower becomes, the more masterful her movements — and the easier it is for her to enter the flow. Technique training and experience allow an advanced follower to completely let go and trust her body to respond naturally, creating the perfect conditions for bliss. For leaders, however, this doesn't always happen. One leader shared that as he advanced in learning complex tango vocabulary and technique, he actually moved further away from enjoying the dance: "The bliss I felt in the first year or two of tango — I can't find it again, no matter how much I chase it." The more complex are the combinations, the more mental effort is often required to lead them.

So what can you do as a leader to find your bliss? The key ideas are to orient yourself toward intrinsic motivation and to bring more of your intuitive brain into play, as followers do. Look for a body practice — yoga, meditation, or Qigong — that helps you become comfortable with and nurture the flow state. Turn your curiosity inward and deepen your body awareness.

I also recommend simplifying your tango vocabulary. Of course, this may sound like heresy if you've invested significant time and money in mastering a long list of figures and transitions. I'm not saying you should throw it all out the window. Rather, I'm suggesting that your bliss may be waiting for you in a different direction. When you replace the quantity of figures with qualities of movements, and when you learn to savor a simple step taken together with your partner to embody the music, you'll find yourself back on the path to what you seek.

Multitasking and the Subconscious Mind

I don't believe Caesar could truly focus on doing 27 things at the same time. If he tried, the outcome would likely have been 27 poor results. In essence, when we dance, we're really doing just one thing. It's only when we break the process down into smaller components, each demanding a fraction of our attention, that we realize how many components there actually are. But we're not really multitasking — dancing is one continuous act that calls for our full attention.

When you're learning, or when you're changing something about your tango, you naturally direct more attention to specific aspects of your dance. For instance, you might focus on releasing tension in your arm. The process of learning, especially in body practices, typically goes through the following stages:

Unconscious incompetence → Conscious incompetence → Conscious competence → Unconscious competence[23]

Let's take the arm tension example. Unconscious incompetence means you're holding tension in your arm without realizing it. Conscious incompetence means you've started to notice it — perhaps once in a while during the dance you become aware of the tension and release it. Conscious competence is when you deliberately direct attention to your arm to keep it toned and relaxed. Unconscious competence is when you've fully succeeded — your arm remains toned and relaxed without any conscious effort. Until the

---

[23] Burch, N. Four Stages of Competence.

change you're working on reaches this final stage, it belongs on your checklist.

In the beginning, paying attention to just one "piece of the puzzle" is usually the most you can handle. But it's rare that you want to change only one thing. More often, you'll need to add several items to your checklist: keeping your head up, minding your axis, breathing voluntarily, and so on. So how do you keep all of this in mind at once? That, too, is a skill — one you can train and develop like a muscle.

Each of us has a wonderful assistant who is always by our side. Most people don't use its services simply because they're not aware of its existence. I'm talking about your subconscious mind. Think of it as a process running quietly in the background of your awareness. It doesn't require much energy, yet it's always doing *something*.

You've likely seen your subconscious in action. For example, when you were considering buying a certain model of car, you suddenly started noticing that same model everywhere on the streets. Those cars were there before your considerations as well — it was your subconscious, having received an unspoken task, that began pointing them out to you.

Since your subconscious is always keeping itself busy, you might as well give it something useful to do. You can assign tasks and directives to it, and before long you'll be pleasantly surprised by the results. Even when you're not paying attention, it will be making subtle changes, small adjustments, and quiet steps toward the goal you've set. The way to engage your subconscious is simple: state clearly what you want to change, whether silently or out loud.

There are a couple of important things to remember when working with your subconscious mind. Always use positive statements when formulating your tasks — your subconscious does not understand negation. In other words, frame your tasks around what you want, not what you don't want. Instead of saying, "I'm working on not tensing my arm and making sure I don't push with my head," say, "I'm working on softening my arm and my neck."

Also, don't try to micromanage your subconscious. It works in the background, behind your direct awareness. Give it your tasks and then let it be. Results may take time to appear, especially when you're just beginning to work this way. State the tasks again, but remain patient.

Think of your subconscious mind as the company's best employee — someone allowed to work on her own schedule, even if that means staring at the ceiling for hours because that's how she finds inspiration. She will do the work on her own terms; your job is simply to trust that she will deliver.

ADD A POINT TO YOUR "CHECKLIST" EXERCISE

At the beginning of a practica, tell your partner the point you want to add to your list of things you're working on. For example, you might say, "I'm working on paying attention to my breath while dancing." This will task your subconscious mind and, at first, direct some of your conscious attention to that point. After a while, your breath may slip out of awareness, and that's ok. Your subconscious will find moments to remind you of it as you dance. This is your progress.

Adding another point to your checklist sends your subconscious to work on incorporating it into your dance. Once this aspect reaches the stage of unconscious competence, it fits naturally into your awareness because it has become part of the one thing you're focused on — it's now part of your dance.

Energy

There's a fascinating story that dates back to the invention of the EEG (electroencephalogram) machine. When scientists discovered that different parts of the brain emit electromagnetic signals of varying strengths at different times, they began gathering this information by placing electrodes on the surface of a subject's head. For a long time, however, they kept encountering a great deal of electromagnetic "noise" during these experiments, and no one could figure out where it was coming from. They tried isolating the testing area from every possible source of interference, but the strange noise persisted.

The mystery was solved when someone placed one electrode on the subject's heart and subtracted its signal from the main input set — the "noise" disappeared. It turned out that the heart's electromagnetic field is so strong and far-reaching that it substantially influenced the data coming from the sensors on the subject's head. This story beautifully illustrates just how much energy our bodies generate — and this is only in terms of electromagnetism.

Each of us has a unique energy signature. If we think of energy in terms of vibrations — again, think *spirals* — then these vibrations have specific geometric qualities. Some of these qualities may be shared among all human beings, while others are uniquely yours. By paying attention to your sixth sense — your perception of energy — you may notice things that science cannot yet fully explain. For example, someone walks in, and the energy of the entire room changes. Or you sense someone standing behind you and somehow know who it is. Our consciousness shapes and molds cosmic energy, making the energy signature of each one of us truly unique.

The brain is usually the first organ we associate with consciousness — it seems to act as the body's "network operations center." But if we carry this analogy further and look at a typical company's network operations center, we won't find the executives there; strategic decisions are made somewhere else. Similarly, in the context of consciousness in the body, the heart is designed to play the executive role.

Here are a few scientific clues that point in this direction: the heart contains about 40,000 neurons, roughly 67% of its cells are nerve cells, and — as the EEG story illustrates — the heart's electromagnetic field is about 5,000 times stronger than that of the brain.

Perhaps a meditative exercise from Tantra will help you experience your body's energy firsthand.

> **"Ring of Light" Exercise**
>
> This partner exercise takes about 15 minutes. Put on the "Om Namah Shivaya" audio chant — I've prepared it for you here: blissfultango.com/ring

blissfultango.com/ring

Sit on the floor with cushions or pillows for comfort, back-to-back with your partner. Both of you should sit in a relaxed version of the lotus position, with your backs touching. The chant is cyclical: one "**OM** Namah Shi**VA**ya" corresponds to one full cycle of breath. Partners breathe in counter-phase to each other — when one is inhaling, the other is exhaling.

The leader begins to inhale on "OM" and to exhale on "VA." The follower begins to exhale on "OM" and to inhale on "VA." Both partners visualize a cluster of light uniformly circulating between them in a continuous ring path. During "OM," visualize the light moving from the follower's heart chakra into the leader's heart chakra, and then down. During "VA," visualize it moving from the leader's root chakra (the perineum) into the follower's root chakra, and then up. Each "Om Namah Shivaya" cycle represents one complete circulation of energy between the two partners.

A more intimate version of this exercise has the partners facing each other, with the follower sitting on the leader's lap and embracing the leader with arms and legs. Either version, however, allows you to feel the energy flowing between you and your partner.

We can consider two types of energy: the energy of your state, which is always there, and the energy of your movement. The energy of your state includes factors like how tired you are, your body temperature, your mood, your heart rate, how tense or relaxed you are, etc. Without moving, it can be difficult to deliberately change this energy — unless you're a Tibetan monk trained in such practices.

By definition, the energy of movement is much more dynamic. Depending on what you want to express, you can vary the qualities of this energy: speed, power, dissipation, softness, percussiveness, spontaneity, and so on. All of these shape the energy of your movement. We will explore movement qualities in more detail in a later chapter.

The key question here is *how* we move. Our state certainly influences the way we move, yet changing the energy of our movement can also shift the energy of our state. Energy, therefore, creates a feedback loop between state and movement, with each continuously shaping the other.

Whether you like it or not, your energy radiates and transmits your state to everyone around you. Energy is a carrier of information. Sensitive people will feel your mood and state while dancing with you. Those who are especially sensitive may even sense it just by standing nearby or seeing you across the room. Trying to hide your state is rarely worth the effort and is usually futile. What can help, however, is to consider the choices we make that directly influence the energy of our state.

It's important to pay attention to your feelings when choosing a potential partner for a tanda. Of course, our personal emotional compass isn't always precise, and sometimes a tanda feels like twelve minutes of waiting for the *cortina*[24]. But if you consistently make yourself dance with people you don't truly want to dance with — whether out of social pressure, guilt, or an inability to say *no* — it will inevitably have a negative impact on your energy.

---

[24] Short non-tango music played between *tandas* to indicate a break and to signal partner change.

What you do regularly has the greatest impact on you. This applies not only to your work and lifestyle choices, but also to the information you consume on daily basis. Just like with food, it's important to be mindful of what you listen to and watch. Some things nourish you, while other things drain you and bring you down. The kind of information you take in — and, most importantly, how it usually makes you feel — has a powerful influence on your health, your state, and your energy.

Energy Mindset

If you explore the nature of reality through the works of Einstein, Schwarzschild, Planck, and Haramein, a fascinating picture begins to emerge. All matter and particles can be seen as *vortices* in the fabric of spacetime at the quantum scale. What was once thought of as "empty space" is, in fact, what Einstein called *ether* — where Planck-scale electromagnetic fluctuations give rise to everything we perceive as reality. From this perspective, the entire Universe is *energy* expressed in countless forms.

Qigong and Tai Chi describe something similar, teaching that the foundation of all existence is cosmic energy. In these traditions, energy flows between a point and infinity, linking every living being with the cosmos. Tantra offers another view, suggesting that our energy originates from our first chakra. These perspectives may all hold truth: the cosmos is filled with energy, and our bodies serve as channels through which it flows. Rather than being the source of energy, we are its conduits.

At one tango marathon I heard two contrasting accounts of energy and became curious about how diversely people understand this subject. It was a Sunday afternoon, that special time when physical exhaustion blends with a saturation of happiness hormones and creates a kind of bliss-on-the-rocks. "I've given everything I could give, I'm done," said one dancer, lounging in the chill-out space. Minutes later another said, "I've received all I wanted to receive, I'm ready to go home."

Both were speaking about the same thing: the exchange of energy that happens at these wonderful events. Their goals were different, and both had fulfilled them before the marathon ended. One came to give — to share their energy with others and enjoy the act of giving. The other came to receive — to find joy in taking in the energy of others.

These examples highlight people's energy mindset — the way we understand energy, its source, and the processes of depletion, recharge, and exchange. Many people see their bodies as *vessels* that can at times be full or empty. Like a battery, the body needs stillness and time — sometimes hours, sometimes days — to recharge. Some dancers see their partners as a source of energy, while others aim to give away all the energy they have.

You can probably imagine the challenges this mindset creates. A "giver" may quickly become drained. A "taker" may leave others feeling depleted, and potential partners might, knowingly or not, avoid their cabeceo. Even if you try to keep the exchange fair, a limited energy mindset will always limit your dance. The essence of dance lies in the unrestrained release of energy. When you set boundaries around your dance, the bliss you are seeking becomes much harder to reach.

An unlimited energy mindset, on the other hand, invites you to give it everything you've got, no matter the circumstances. When you see your body not as a vessel but as a *conduit* directly connected to an infinite source, both your self-perception and your psychology begin to transform. Giving and receiving energy feels as natural as breathing in and out. There is no need to keep track of fairness in the exchange — just as you don't measure how much air you inhale or exhale. Gratitude arises for everything you receive, and your generosity flows effortlessly, because you feel you are already overflowing with energy.

Your psychology and self-perception have a direct impact on your physiology — your body adapts to your perspectives. Your mindset strongly influences the way your body functions, since you are constantly creating a vibrational environment that's rooted in your beliefs. An unlimited energy mindset transforms how you feel: you won't tire as quickly, your overall energy will increase, and you won't feel drained no matter with whom you dance. The body always finds resources for the tasks you give it, so the more energy you share, the more it is replenished.

A wonderful tanguera friend once asked me at a marathon, "Tell me something. When I come to a milonga, I look at the dance floor, I see that Aleksey is already dancing. When I'm on the dance floor, and I look around, I see that Aleksey is dancing nearby. When I'm resting on the couch and I look at the dance floor, I see that Aleksey is still dancing. What's your secret?" I suspect that my perspective on energy has something to do with it.

Of course, I still get tired, and I take breaks. We are physical beings with real physical and chemical limits, no matter what we believe. We all need time to recharge. The real questions are: "How much time do you need to recharge?" "What helps you recharge?" and "How often do you need it?" Each of us will answer differently. You can experiment with these parameters and discover what works best for you. Still, regardless of your resting patterns, I can assure you that the main factor determining how much energy you have will be your mindset.

How Much of Yourself Are You Giving?

Our bodies are remarkably smart. Without us even noticing, they are constantly optimizing internal processes. This optimization is aimed, first and foremost, at conserving energy. While this makes perfect sense biologically, an important question arises when you dance: How much of yourself are you giving in this moment?

Subconsciously, we adjust the amount of energy we're willing to expend based on how important we perceive the situation to be. Imagine you're about to give a presentation you've been preparing for weeks. Much depends on you being fully focused and bringing your best into the room, so you'll likely operate at close to 100% of your potential. Now compare that to doing a simple household chore. How much focus, attention, and energy do you really need to vacuum the house? 19%? It's enough, as long as it gets the job done.

The trouble is that we often rank the importance of a situation while dancing and give only a corresponding fraction of ourselves to the experience. Maybe you're dancing with a beginner, or it's just a practica, or it's late at night — your subconscious will find reasons to lower the importance of the moment and reduce your energy output to a minimum. And then what's the point of dancing if you're giving it only 23%?

When you hold back, you end up shirking, slacking, and cutting corners. By downplaying the importance of your dance, you effectively close the door to the euphoria you're seeking.

How do you give your all to the dance? Dissociate more, add energy to your dissociation. I know only a few followers who put extra energy into their dissociation during a giro — it feels divine for the leader, making their turns unforgettable. Engage your abs, obliques, and back, stretch your spirals, project your leg, push the floor. Reframe tango as an activity to which you *want* to give the entirety of yourself. Much like in a romantic relationship, tango will give you more than you ever dreamed of if you give it everything you've got.

Emotions

If you ask someone, "What are you feeling now?" chances are they'll begin their answer with, "I *think* I'm feeling…" The mind, in its constant attempts to moderate and control everything — as amusing as that may be — has inadvertently become the warden of our emotional state.

You're probably familiar with the concept of the Intelligence Quotient, or I.Q. Our world seems obsessed with intelligence, as if it were the ultimate key to life. But there is also E.Q. — the Emotional Quotient — which focuses on our ability to feel, process, and express emotions. Unfortunately, emotional intelligence receives far less attention in our society. As a result, many people face a significant problem: they're not expressing their emotions.

How this came about is fairly clear. Our world constantly encourages us to hide, downplay, and suppress our emotions. It's considered impolite to laugh out loud in public; if someone is crying, we tend to assume something is wrong with them. Other people's emotions are often treated as unwelcome — as a nuisance or even as aggression. These unspoken rules of etiquette leave few opportunities for people to release emotional energy and truly express themselves. When emotional energy is left unexpressed, it remains in the body and becomes toxic, showing up — in the best case — as muscle knots.

Feelings are frequently contrasted with logic and reasoning, and portrayed as superfluous and irrational. In many modern films, the heroine's "biggest mistake" is often shown as a decision guided by her emotions. But is that really true?

What is the purpose of our emotions? They are not a random evolutionary accident. On the contrary, like the other systems in our bodies, our emotions are a technology so advanced that we still don't fully understand it. Emotions serve as our compass[25] — our personal navigation system — always pointing toward "true north," the highest good. To use this system, all we need to do is turn inward and pay attention to how we feel in any given moment.

Being guided by your feelings doesn't mean going to extremes, throwing fits, or becoming a slave to your emotions. On the contrary, such behavior indicates that this person is out of touch with

---

[25] Hicks, E. & Hicks, J. The Astonishing Power of Emotions: Let Your Feelings Be Your Guide. Hay House Inc., 2007.

their emotions. Being guided by your feelings means consciously choosing your behavior based on what you feel right now.

Isn't it self-centered to be guided only by your own feelings? What about the feelings of other people? Of course, "it takes two." By cultivating your capacity to feel, you can learn not only to sense your own emotions but also the emotions of those around you. Highly empathetic people are on the other side of this spectrum — empaths tend to feel the emotions of other people so strongly that they struggle to distinguish other people's emotions from their own. No matter where you are on this scale, directing your attention inward and using your personal navigation system is an indispensable skill.

Science has shown that people usually make decisions emotionally, and only afterwards justify them with logic — not the other way around. The goal of advertising, for example, is to prompt someone to make a decision based on emotions that were carefully prepared by the marketing team. Someone disconnected from their emotional guidance system and relying solely on reasoning becomes an easy target for manipulation. Focusing only on logic narrows your vision, and this is precisely the blind spot that manipulators exploit.

Do you ever wonder why some people experience far more drama in their personal lives than others? Over and over again: a different partner, different circumstances, the same lesson. Many don't realize that they are the screenwriter, the director, the lead actor, and the audience in each repeating "episode" of their life.

So why the unwanted encounters? One possible cause is past trauma. Unaware of the traumatic effect a previous experience has created, people may be drawn back into similar circumstances in an unconscious attempt to remedy the wound. Sadly, the effect is often the opposite — they end up retraumatized.

Another possibility is that the need to experience and express dramatic emotions drives a person to create, involuntarily, the very conditions that fulfill this need.

We will look at trauma more closely in a later chapter. For now, consider this question: how do you satisfy the need to experience dramatic emotions? Awareness of the need itself is key. There are two separate aims here: one is to meet a need, and the other is to pursue what you truly want in life. To move toward what you truly want, you must first clarify it for yourself and then focus on it to such a degree that nothing else can come your way.

As for satisfying the need for drama — well, this is where social tango, with its countless opportunities to experience and express every imaginable emotion, truly shines. Choose a particularly dramatic tanda, let it all out on the dance floor — an important note here is that we direct our emotional energy not at our partner, but at the floor — then walk away, leaving all the drama behind. The word "satisfied" doesn't even begin to describe your state after a tanda like that: "I feel like I need a cigarette, and I don't even smoke!" Resolve, vulnerability and openness in the face of the heaviest emotions can result in the peak-of-your-experience, seventh-heaven euphoria.

Your exploration of the emotional spectrum will likely heighten your sensitivity and awareness of both your own feelings and those of others. You may even begin to notice the emotional component in places and situations where you wouldn't have expected it before.

Emotional sensitivity is a quality you can develop and practice — and emotions, without a doubt, are one of the pathways to bliss.

Embodying the Music

Consider the different levels at which we can process music in our bodies: hearing, listening to, feeling and embodying the music.

1) Hearing the music is simply registering the fact that sound is present. Like noticing peripheral noise, hearing happens in the background while your attention is elsewhere.
2) Listening to music requires directing some of your attention to the music. Listening is the active form of hearing. When you listen to music, you may recognize the composition. At this level you're more engaged, but there is still a clear separation between you and the music, which remains outside of you.
3) Feeling the music means being drawn into the composition. You let the music inside, and it begins to affect your emotional state. The key distinction here is that your focused attention evokes an emotional response.
4) Embodying the music is when you let the composition in so deeply that you yield some of your cognitive control and allow the music to initiate and guide your movements. This is the active form of feeling the music. Embodying the music means surrendering your body to the music. Of course, you don't lose control — you maintain principal command. Embodying the music creates a trance-like state in which you willingly give part of your control to the music. *Trance* is the key word here; this is the level we ultimately want to reach.

> **EMBODYING THE MUSIC WITH ECSTATIC DANCE EXERCISE**
>
> When you're alone in the comfort of your own space, put on any music you feel like moving to — it doesn't have to be tango. For the duration of one track, let go of technique, aesthetics, and structure. Your only limits are your body's natural range of movement and the space around you. No one is watching, so set yourself free. Consciously surrender control of your body — or as much of it as you can — to the music. Take on the role of an observer and maintain an attitude of curiosity.

The variety of moods in tango music spans the entire emotional spectrum. Joy, sadness, anger, romance, melancholy, humor — name an emotion, and an experienced DJ can put together a tanda that evokes it. Simply by listening to a tango composition, you can sense its emotional charge and place it somewhere along the spectrum. To embody the music, you must be willing to step fully into the emotion this piece offers and genuinely feel what comes up for you in the process.

Easier said than done! Many people have entire "off-limits" zones on their emotional palette. I know this because I was one of them until a certain point in my tango adolescence, when I realized it no longer served me. Past traumatic experiences often make it deeply uncomfortable — even unbearable — to truly feel certain emotions, whether anger, playfulness, or anything else. Here, again, you face a choice: you can continue to avoid uncomfortable emotions, or you can treat them as opportunities for personal growth. Some of life's greatest rewards — ease, freedom, and lightness — are hidden precisely where it's uncomfortable for you to look. All it takes to reach these rewards is your willingness to recognize your "off-limits" zones and your courage to be uncomfortable for a while.

Why not simply neglect one or two emotional zones if you're comfortable with all the rest? Bliss has a strong emotional component. The key to bringing this part of the puzzle into harmony is your emotional wholeness — your acceptance and integration of *all* emotions. Without emotional integrity, reaching bliss can be difficult, and here's why.

"Off-limits" zones imply danger. The same psychological mechanism that keeps you from stepping into these "danger zones" will likely also hold you back from wandering into bliss. When you make peace with every part of yourself — when you own the entirety of who you are — you naturally release those safety mechanisms and let go of what once limited and blocked you. The freedom that follows becomes fertile ground for the euphoria you seek.

FEEL THE "OFF LIMITS" EMOTION OF A TANGO COMPOSITION EXERCISE

Find a tango composition you *don't* enjoy dancing to specifically because of its emotional content. Play the recording while sitting comfortably, and pay close attention to the feelings it stirs in you. Breathe consciously, as this helps catalyze any psycho-emotional process. Closing your eyes may also help by keeping out distractions. Notice how your body responds to the emotion. Where do you feel discomfort? Going deep into an "off-limits" emotion will likely bring up past experiences or trauma. When this happens, you'll gain insight into which memories are holding you back. Afterwards, you'll have the chance to work through them using whatever healing modality you prefer.

Emotions are a peculiar beast — both universal and unique. They're universal because most people can feel sadness, for example, and unique because each of us experiences emotions differently. Not only is my sadness different from your sadness, but the sadness I feel today is not the same as the sadness I felt yesterday, even under similar circumstances. Our movements in dance share this quality: they're both universal and uniquely our own.

"Emotion is Energy in Motion"
—Bashar

VISUALIZE THE EMOTIONS OF A TANGO COMPOSITION EXERCISE

Put on a particularly emotional composition, sit back, and get comfortable. Close your eyes to shut out distractions. Focus on the music and notice the feelings that surface. Now visualize a sphere floating in empty space. Let the music shape this picture and fill in the details — imagine the sphere as a reflection of the music's emotions.

Stay curious: How big is the sphere? What colors does it take on? What is its texture? Notice how these qualities shift as the composition unfolds. Is the sphere moving? Shaking? Floating weightlessly? How do its movements change? Does its shape transform? What happens to its surface? Allow your visualization to reveal just how varied and eccentric the emotional dynamics of a tango composition can be.

Argentine tango offers a perfect opportunity to feel, embody, and express almost any emotion you choose. Simply by listening to a composition, you can sense its emotional charge. Dancing takes it further — when you dance, you not only express those emotions but also release them, letting them go. This is freedom.

At the end of an especially playful or wild composition, it's not uncommon to hear laughter ripple through the milonga. There were instances, when my partner and I left the dance floor with tears in our eyes.

If you want a tanda to be memorable, it has to be emotional. That's how our memory works — emotions are the custodians of memory. A single emotional moment from childhood can stay with you for the rest of your life, while an ordinary day fades from your memory as soon as it's over. The choice is yours.

At this stage of my tango journey, the process of feeling the music's emotion begins almost involuntarily. As soon as a composition starts playing at a milonga, I tend to surrender fully to its emotion. Whatever I'm feeling is usually written plainly on my face. Together, these tendencies have led to some funny moments around the dance floor.

Once, during a cortina, I was talking with a tanguera when a particularly gloomy tanda began. She looked at me mid-sentence and asked, "Oh no! Did I say something wrong?" Not at all — it's the music.

Story

"Always tell your story with your dance." I felt my tango teacher's words sink deep into my core, changing me. What are we, if not stories the Universe is telling itself? A story is an experience — woven from situations, choices, actions, and emotions. An engaging story draws the listener in. Without even realizing it, the listener identifies with the hero, makes difficult choices, and experiences the events vicariously. A good story changes the listener in a way that's somewhat similar to actually having lived it.

Hearing *Confesión* always takes me back to a deeply emotional moment in my life, when a girl and I were saying goodbye. We danced this Troilo-Ruiz tanda, and *Confesión* — with lyrics that seemed to mirror what was happening between us, wrapped in a somber mood — etched itself into me, leaving an emotional imprint for the rest of my life.

Like a story, every tango composition has a beginning, a middle, and an end. In tango classes you were probably taught that it's important to finish a composition well — on time, and fully stopped in a comfortable "ending" pose. An experienced tanguera friend used to tease me whenever I repeated the same ending from one composition to the next: "¡Finales diferentes!" — different endings! And she was right. How you end a composition matters greatly, because it's what you and your partner take with you when leaving the dance floor. The ending creates the aftertaste of your dance.

What many dancers overlook is that the beginning of your dance is just as important. The way you start — especially the first composition with a new partner — sets the tone for the entire tanda. Look at it this way: if a film begins with bad acting, would you want to keep watching, even if the trailer looked promising? Begin telling your story well. Focus on the embrace. Take a few seconds to connect with your partner. Breathe in and out together, then listen to the music *as a couple*. The music will always be there.

Every good story has its essential components lined up: the setup, the shake-up, the games, the culmination, and the resolution. In much the same way, every tango composition carries progression — it does not maintain the same emotion from beginning to end. If you listen closely, you'll notice the emotions shifting as the piece unfolds. An engaging film takes you on a rollercoaster of feelings, leaving you with the sense of having lived an entire life in the hero's shoes, even though it has only been two hours. What makes a film memorable are the emotional shifts that unfold within each scene. In the same way, you can notice and embody the emotional changes within a tango composition to create a dance that feels alive and deeply engaging.

The story you dance doesn't have to come from your own life. You might choose to dance the story of the composition, or even a different story altogether, which resonates with you emotionally in this particular moment. What matters is that you reach for the meaning — the essence of your in-the-moment experience — and express it in your dance. Bring your unique emotional perspective to this musical moment. Of course, these meanings aren't found on the surface. The depth of your search for essence and meaning is entirely up to you. There are no limits. An experiential immersion like this is undoubtedly one of the pathways to bliss.

Musicality

Musicality in tango is a combination of choices. Some fit the moment better than others. Everything we do on the dance floor — figures, steps, *embellishments*[26], timing, and qualities of movement — comes from the choices we continuously make. Here I would like to focus on qualities of movement, because this subject, while very important, is rarely addressed. If you ignore what the music offers and fail to vary the qualities of your movements, then your polished to perfection figures and steps will feel robotic. If a crying moment of Troilo's *Confesión* is given the same movement qualities of a *sacada*[27], as the low-and-slow churning of Pugliese's *Locura Tanguera*, then in both cases the figure will feel lifeless and sterile in its uniformity.

It's the variation of movement qualities that lets us express the full palette of moods and emotions in different tango compositions. By varying the way we move, we can turn the richness of tango music into the richness of our dance.

In a previous life, I played drums and percussion in a folk-rock band. When we were learning one of Anastasia's new songs, she said something simple yet beautiful: "Now that we have the structure down, let's work on the dynamics." The structure of a composition is the order of its parts; dynamics are the subtler variations of intensity, volume, and timing — the accents, quiet notes, swing, the ebb

---

[26] Same as *adorno*, a decorative movement added to steps or figures.
[27] A move where one dancer's leg displaces and steps into the space of the partner's free leg.

and flow of energy. And these are just a few of the many qualities of sound.

Fortunately, tango music offers an immense range of sound qualities. Below, we'll explore some movement characteristics and how they can be used to express different qualities of sound. But first, let's consider something very basic.

What's in a step? We often think of a single step as something elementary, indivisible. Yet a step, aside from engaging hundreds of muscles throughout the body, can also be viewed as a sequence of overlapping stages: preparation, push, projection, landing, transfer of weight, release, and arrival.

To simplify, we can group these into three parts: the beginning, middle, and end of the movement — corresponding roughly to the attack, sustain, and decay of a sound.

Mapping Music to Movement

At its core, sound is movement — it is the propagation of waves through a medium. What sets one sound apart from another are its qualities, the subtle differences in the patterns of their waves. Musicality in movement, then, is your delving deep into discerning these subtleties so you can visualize, conceptualize, and feel the underlying geometry of sound. The most direct way to approach musicality in tango is to translate the geometry of sound into the geometry of your movement.

What is the geometry of sound? The waveforms shown on sound-editing software hint at it, but the picture is incomplete. Sound is three-dimensional by nature, radiating outward from its source in longitudinal waves. Its true "shape" is a series of concentric spheres, each with the sound source at its center (left).

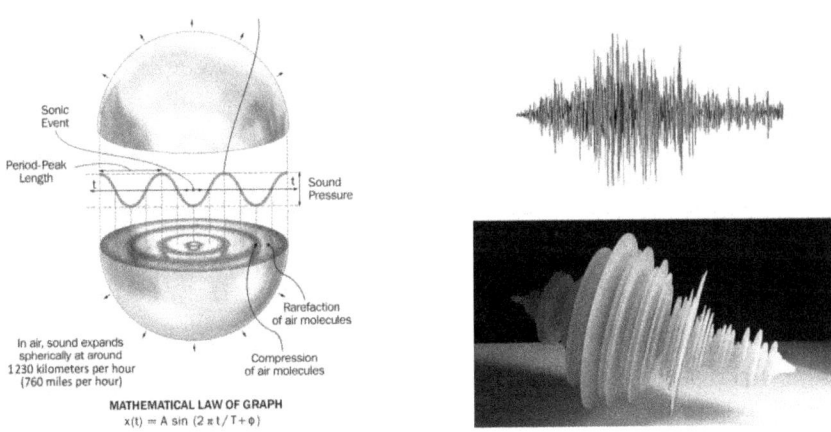

For our purposes, however, it may be easier to imagine sound as a three-dimensional spiral with varying radii. The image on the right shows one such 3D example extruded from a two-dimensional waveform, the likes of which are shown in sound-editing programs.

The first property of tango music we can look at is the distinction between sounds that are more discrete and those that are more analog. Discrete sounds — a staccato piano chord, a sharp attack of a bandoneón, the pluck of a bass string — map neatly onto steps. Analog sounds — an unending violin note, a singer's sustained tone — invite movements that are smoother and more flowing, rarely suggesting so much as a weight change.

Of course, these concepts aren't black and white. Like yin and yang, each contains a trace of the other. Discrete events still have analog qualities, like amplitude and duration. Analog events are also, in a subtle way, discrete, since every sound has a beginning and an end.

Each movement of your body, like each sound in tango music, contains both of these qualities. What places them closer to one side of the spectrum or the other are their individual characteristics. After all, tango movements are both discrete (steps) and analog (spirals).

Here are some additional properties of both movement and sound, along with ideas on how they may correlate:

Size – The size of a step can reflect the "size" of a sound, primarily its volume. If you imagine a sound as a three-dimensional spiral, it will have a certain length and diameter. How big or small are these dimensions? Is the sound grand and expansive, or faint and barely audible? Some sounds are so "small" that translating them into regular-sized steps would not feel musical. Conversely, your technique should enable you to take a large step, regardless of your physique.

Pitch – Where is this sound in tonality compared to those before and after it? Is the pitch rising or falling? I like to play with vertical levels here: a lower pitch can be expressed with a lower vertical level, while a higher pitch reaches upward. Of course, reversing this can also be fun.

Acceleration – Is the sound speeding up or slowing down? A striking example of an accelerating note, called *latigo* (whip), appears at the start of certain phrases in Demare's *Una emoción*, where the violin accelerates while climbing in pitch. This quality translates beautifully into acceleration and deceleration of movement. It can shape the beginning of a step, its ending, or both. An accelerating sound, for instance, can be expressed with a "throwing" quality of movement — since throwing is, at its core, acceleration in action.

Weight – Does the note hit your chest like a sledgehammer in Pugliese's *La Yumba*, or is it feather-light and soft, like in Fresedo's *Canto de Amor*? I tend to accent heavy sounds in the landing stage of a step. Lighter sounds — especially when they appear for just a few bars, as in Pugliese's instrumental interludes — can be expressed through an emphasis on lightness in the upper body, a softening of the embrace, and a flowing quality of movement.

Mass – How much substance is in the sound? How far can you shift your center of mass away from your axis during rotation? When you play with this, your free leg can feel as if it weighs a ton — lower register sounds beg for this — or it can feel as light as a feather.

Texture – Is the sound coarse, like the "laughing" violin's *chicharra*, or velvety smooth? Does it make you want to drag your heel (or the side of your shoe) against the parquet, or does it create the sensation of floating above the dance floor? Is it a long sound made of multiple consecutive strikes of a single piano key? All of this contributes to texture — and we're only scratching the surface here.

Tension – Does the sound make your body tighten and wind up like a spring, or does it invite you to soften and relax? Notes played slightly ahead of the beat, notes that are played in a slightly higher pitch, dissonant chords — all generate tension. Osvaldo Pugliese's *La Cachila* (1945) is a vivid example of this, especially around 0:43.

Viscosity – Does the sound make you feel as if you're moving through honey, your every movement slowed to a crawl? Sometimes a single viscous step can stretch across an entire measure — or even several measures of music.

Energy – Is the sound building energy or is the singer practically whispering? Do you feel compelled to move, or do you need to slow down and breathe? The energy of sound is usually a blend of speed and volume, and it can be mapped to movement in the same way.

Swing – Is the sound played "late," almost colliding with the notes that follow? In tango, vocals often carry this quality. Swing notes can be expressed by slightly delaying the corresponding movement.

Duration – Is the sound cut short, or does it ring out? A long note — often appearing at the end of a phrase — can be emphasized by pausing before the next phrase, letting the note linger.

Accent – Is the sound marked in a way that sets it apart from those before it? Musicians often accent notes by playing them with more energy. Similar to long notes, I sometimes like to mark accented notes with a subsequent pause, even when the next part has already begun.

Attack – Does the sound hit, or does it slowly materialize out of thin air? This quality at the start of a sound maps directly to the beginning of a movement.

Mood – Is the sound melancholy or playful? Is it angry or dreamy? Whatever the movement, you can "color" it with any mood that fits the sound.

Uniformity – Is the sound coherent and steady throughout, or do its qualities shift as it unfolds? Your movement can change in the same way, evolving at any moment during its lifespan.

This is by no means an exhaustive list of sound qualities that can be translated into their movement counterparts. These fundamental attributes often combine to create more complex behaviors that belong equally to sound and to movement. Tango music is full of moments where a sound can be exploded, dragged, smeared, smashed, kneaded, churned, nudged, touched, flicked, cuddled, enveloped, caressed, tickled, floated, glided, turned, twisted, splashed — the list goes on.

There are also dualistic qualities: a sound can be thrown or caught, pushed or pulled, opened or closed, submerged or revealed, breathed in or breathed out, wound up or unwound, suspended or dropped, launched or screeched to a halt, called or answered, brought to the foreground or hidden in the back. Some patterns span multiple notes in succession: series, scales, cycles, waves, reversals, zigzags, and more. All of these attributes, behaviors, and patterns are, by definition, qualities of movement.

It's up to you to embody these qualities and weave them into your dance in whatever way feels right. When the qualities of your steps align with the qualities of the music, your dance will always be musical. Even at a crowded milonga, when there's no space to take a step, you can still dance weight changes in a way, which will brilliantly express the energy of the composition.

> ### DANCE WITHOUT TAKING A SINGLE STEP EXERCISE
>
> Pick a playful composition, such as Aníbal Troilo's *Yo Soy El Tango* (1941), and dance to it with your partner in the following way — imagine you're at the most crowded milonga, where neither of you can take a single step. Use only weight changes, play with dissocia-

> tion and levels. Allow the energy of the music to come through despite this restriction. Get creative. Redirect the urge to take a step into embodying the music's energy in place.

How can you discern and develop qualities of movement? First, by truly listening to a variety of tango music[28] and allowing yourself to feel the emotions it carries. During the next tanda you sit out, close your eyes and simply notice: What is the emotional tone of this moment? What emotion is the singer experiencing right now? Without feeling and embodying genuine emotion, the movement qualities described above will remain superficial — even if they happen to match the music.

Second, watch video recordings of tango orchestras — both the original masters and contemporary bands. Pay close attention to the movements of the musicians' arms and hands; these gestures reveal the inherent dance of the instruments. What is the sound of an acoustic instrument? It is the musician's state — his mood and emotions — translated through the contraction and release of his muscle groups, which produce movement. That movement activates the instrument, and the instrument produces sound.

And what is dance? It is the dancer's state — her mood and emotions — translated through the contraction and release of her muscle groups, which produce movement. In this way, tango orchestras become a perfect model for exploring qualities of movement in your own dance. If there is a conductor — like the great D'Arienzo conducting *Loca* — pay attention to his hands and the qualities of his

---

[28] https://argentinetangoradio.com/
https://radiotangouno.pl/

movements. Later, on the dance floor, you will have a somewhat refined reference to the sound's inherent movement, making it easier to translate the qualities of tango music into the qualities of your dance.

Third, try visualizing a sound as an object moving through space. How does the object behave as it travels? Just as important, how does its behavior *change* along the way? Notice the beginning, middle, and end of a sound. Each stage matters, and each relates to the stages of your body's movement through space.

The beauty of these qualities is that they affect more than a single step — they affect your entire body. When embodied, they can shift your whole state of being many times over within a single composition, if you surrender to the emotions of the music.

For most tango orchestras and compositions, the attack of a sound maps naturally to the landing stage of a step. This works well in medium- and fast-tempo pieces. Slow and grandiose tangos, however — like Carlos Di Sarli's later works — call for something different. In these tangos the sounds are not only "large," but their sustain is powerful and overwhelming. This unique combination of sound dynamics is often better expressed when the attack of a sound is mapped to the earlier, push stage of your step.

> **MAPPING MUSIC TO THE PUSH STAGE OF YOUR STEP**
>
> Walk with your partner to Carlos Di Sarli's *A La Gran Muñeca*, using only forward steps for leaders and back steps for followers. Focus on the beginning — the attack of each beat — as the moment you push off the floor with your standing foot. Notice how this

> changes the qualities of your tango walk. How does it affect the size of your step?

Mindful Movement

What is the difference between a reaction and a response? A reaction happens automatically, on its own. In a reaction there are no alternatives — "A" causes "B." A response, on the other hand, indicates volition — there is a choice. A response is a display of active involvement in the interaction, a presence of intelligence.

The same distinction applies to "autopilot" versus mindful movement. Many leaders and followers often slip into autopilot on the dance floor without realizing it. Certain moves and sequences become so ingrained in a dancer's repertoire that they start acting as filler, inserting themselves into the dance on their own. Completing the *box*[29], repeating the same *adorno*[30] at the end of every *ocho*[31], or leading a *rock step*[32] whenever beginning a turn to the left (my personal nemesis for a long time) — the list of filler moves is long. The symptoms may look different, but the root cause is the same: habitual automatism.

---

[29] A basic step pattern forming a square, useful for beginners to learn structure and rhythm.
[30] Same as *embellishment*, a decorative movement added to steps or figures.
[31] A pivoting step where the dancer traces a figure-eight pattern on the floor.
[32] A quick forward/back weight change (same as *Rebound* and *Rebote*)

How do you break a bad habit? The first step is simply *wanting* to notice the habits in your own dance. Without your genuine desire to notice your habitual motions, they will remain unchanged.

The second step is awareness: pay close attention and notice exactly what your habitual movements are. If you can identify a pattern in your behavior, you can change it.

The third step is to notice the positions and movements that *precede* your habitual motion. This allows you to catch the moment before the automatic motion takes over — and to make a different choice instead.

> **EXCLUDING ONE HABITUAL MOVEMENT EXERCISE**
>
> Do this with a partner at a práctica. Choose one of your habitual movements and set a personal goal for an entire composition to *not* dance this specific move. You're allowed to mess up — what matters is noticing when it happens. You can even stop mid-motion if you catch yourself; after all, you're at a práctica. Simplify. Slow down. Pay attention to the positions and movements that lead into your habitual patterns, and explore what alternative choices are available in those moments.

Move only when something would be missing in the musical moment if you remained still. Of course, this is a maxim, but it carries an important reminder: move only when the music implores you to move. Every movement should have a purpose. If there's a pause in the music, that's your cue not to push through a sequence.

This leads to an essential point: you must be able to stop at any moment during your figures, adornos, and sequences. If you can't, it's time to work on your balance, take technique classes, and examine your "unstoppable" figures closely — because something is likely off there.

Safety on the dance floor always takes precedence over everything else. At a milonga there are other couples around you, and their navigation can be unpredictable. Right or wrong doesn't matter — safety is your responsibility, whether you lead or follow. If your repertoire includes figures or adornos that you cannot stop mid-way, your dancing poses a safety hazard.

"Musical Chairs" Exercise

You probably know the game of musical chairs, where everyone scrambles for a seat when the music stops. This exercise works in a similar way. You'll need a third person to start and stop the music while you and your partner dance. The difference is that when the music stops, instead of searching for a chair, your goal is to stop instantly. Don't finish a sequence, don't complete a step — simply freeze and stand still, exactly as you are in that moment.

Paced acceleration and deceleration illustrate control. The relationship between mindful movement and inertia is similar to that between intelligence and thinking. Mindful movement can incorporate and use inertia, but inertia is only one of its tools. Focused attention and conscious choice of motion are the cornerstones of mindful movement.

Tango music varies widely in terms of accent dynamics — the interplay between "fast" and "slow" passages. This isn't the same as a change in tempo, which you sometimes hear in Osvaldo Pugliese's compositions. Accent dynamics instead refer to the rise and fall in the frequency of accented chords.

> **LISTEN FOR THE ACCENT DYNAMICS EXERCISE**
>
> Listen to *Te Aconsejo Que Me Olvides* by Aníbal Troilo with Francisco Fiorentino. Notice how the frequency of accents changes — some phrases feel "fast," others "slow," even though the tempo stays constant. In some of the "slow" phrases, the instruments still carry the rhythm, but it's hidden in the background, almost inaudible.
>
> Below are two sections of the *variación*[33] beginning around 1:54 — one "fast" and one "slow." The vertical lines mark the accented notes, showing how densely or sparsely they appear in each part.

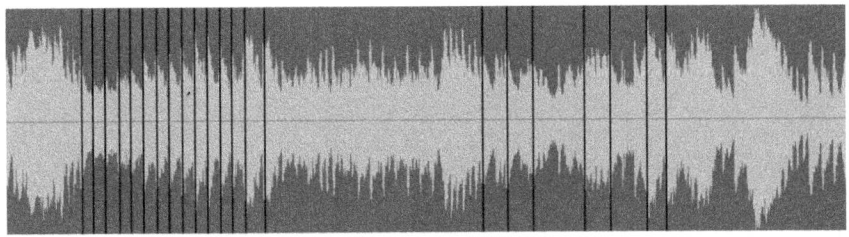

If you dance an entire composition at the same speed, your dance will feel monotone. Adjusting your pace — slowing down or speeding up to reflect the music's accent dynamics — is a key part of musicality.

---

[33] An instrumental section with increased intensity, often used for dynamic or dramatic movement.

Another idea we touched on earlier is the relationship between the size of movement and the size of sound. Nearly every tango composition includes volume dynamics — *crescendo*[34] and *decrescendo*[35]. How loud is this passage? Are the musicians pushing their instruments to the limit, or is the singer barely whispering? Ideally, the volume dynamics of a composition translate into the size of your movements — are you taking large steps, or are you barely moving?

> **LISTEN FOR THE VOLUME DYNAMICS EXERCISE**
>
> Listen to *Torrente* by Aníbal Troilo with Alberto Marino. Notice how the volume varies throughout the composition, sometimes quite dramatically. These changes can also be gradual.
>
> Below is a depiction of an instrumental interlude and a verse beginning around 2:42. While volume dynamics usually play out over shorter spans of time, this segment clearly illustrates the contrast in the "size" of the sound — its volume — highlighted here by the "height" of the sound wave.

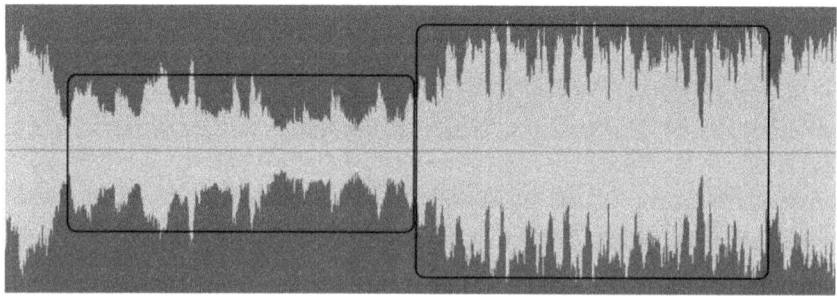

---

[34] An increase in the intensity or volume of sound.
[35] A decrease in the intensity or volume of sound.

In beginner and intermediate classes, your teacher probably told you to make sure every step in the *molinete*[36] is the same size. That stage of technique training is important: it ensures proper dissociation and helps you avoid bad habits, like cutting short your back step.

Once you move beyond that stage, you can begin refining your sensitivity to step size — sensitivity to the lead if you're following, and sensitivity to the music if you're leading. Put simply, if all your steps are the same size, your dance will feel mechanical. Musicality emerges when the volume dynamics of a composition are reflected in the volume dynamics of your movement.

Pauses

In tango music, there aren't many well-known compositions with completely silent pauses. More often the pauses are suggestive, with the last note still ringing, or an instrument quietly carrying a note. A pause doesn't mean you must be absolutely still, but at the very least it calls for slowing down. A pause in the music means that you should not be taking any steps. A slowdown might look like a spiral continuing to unwind slowly. But avoid trying to "fill the airtime." You want your dance to be authentic self-expression, not filler.

---

[36] A turning sequence combining forward, side, and back steps around the partner.

So what exactly are pauses in tango music? It's easier to recognize them when you know what you're looking for. Similar to sounds, we can attribute certain qualities to pauses:

Still pause – a quiet moment when no instruments are playing.

Ringing pause – the last note continues to carry or fades slowly.

Muted pause – the instruments keep playing, but at a much lower volume, almost inaudible.

Vocal pause – only the singer's voice carries a note.

Low energy pause – a pause that invites you to exhale and focus on your partner in close embrace.

High energy pause – a pause that prompts you to inhale, preparing for an energetic passage that follows.

Rising pause – a pause that gently builds anticipation, drawing you upward as you inhale in the moments leading up to it, as heard in *Romance de Barrio* by Aníbal Troilo with Floreal Ruiz.

In terms of geometry, a pause is where a musical spiral ends. There are abrupt pauses in tango music, in which the spiral is cut off, but these cases are rare. Most of the time a pause is where the musical spiral closes, concludes and comes to a point.

Without pauses, speech turns into an unintelligible torrent of words. In the same way, without pauses, tango turns into an incoherent torrent of figures. Unfortunately, this is all too common on the social dance floor. Thoughtfully placed slowdowns and pauses give your dance character and depth.

If a leader proceeds with the next figure without even slowing down between phrases, it won't feel musical to the follower. And if a follower adds an embellishment simply because the leader isn't moving, the leader may wonder whether the two of you are hearing the same music.

> "The secret of tango is in this moment of improvisation that happens between step and step. It is to make the impossible thing possible: to dance silence. This is essential to learn in tango dance, the real dance, that of the silence…"
> —Carlos Gavito

An important gift of pauses is that they let you rest. One of the secrets to stamina is knowing how to space out your breaks. Without rest, you might not even last two hours — let alone a six-hour milonga at a marathon. If you're not feeling a particular tanda, or the partner you hoped to invite is dancing with someone else, embrace this as an opportunity to take a twelve-minute break. Similarly, during the dance, welcome each pause — long or short — as a chance to rest and breathe. Run a mental scan through your body and release any tension you may be holding. These mini-breaks may seem small, but they add up to make a big difference in your overall state.

Savor the pauses. Shift your attention to the embrace, to the sensation of holding your partner, to the feelings in your own body. When you do this, no pause will ever feel awkward, even if it cuts into the next phrase. Take a deeper breath together with your partner. Try to sense what your partner is feeling. Pauses in tango are rarely long, but those one or two seconds can be filled with magic. When you slow down with the music, you slow down time itself, creating a feeling of absence of time and space. *That* is the bliss you're after.

Phrases

Astronomical cycles and biorhythms have a fractal nature: the whole reflects the shape of its parts. Most books, for instance, are divided into chapters, chapters into paragraphs, paragraphs into sentences, and sentences into words. Nature divides everything into smaller units that resemble the whole, and tango is no exception. In tango, not only is a milonga divided into tandas, and tanda into compositions, but the composition is also divided into *phrases*. Slowdowns and pauses, which, like punctuation marks, divide the dance into phrases, are just as important as the stop at the end of a composition.

So, what is a phrase in tango music? A phrase usually consists of eight strong beats, or four measures. In terms of vocals, this often corresponds to four short lines of lyrics. But rather than counting beats, I encourage you to listen for a *statement* that the music makes with a phrase — a complete thought that stands on its own like a sentence. A tango phrase often ends with a punctuation mark — the accent. Resembling the overall composition as a small fractal of the whole, each phrase has its own beginning, middle, and end.

How can you shift your focus to dancing the phrases? And how do you avoid finding yourself halfway through a *lapiz*[37]-enrosque when the phrase ends? Here are a few ideas.

---

[37] A decorative foot movement that traces circular shapes on the floor.

On the conceptual side, start by feeling the phrases in tango music. Learn to recognize their beginnings, middles, and ends. Phrases can be vocal or instrumental, and they often vary from one to the next. Each phrase is as essential as a sentence, and its meaning is lost without punctuation.

On the technical side, simplify your dance. Enjoy your movement together. Walk. Simple steps taken to music will always feel better than a complicated sequence that runs over the end of a phrase, no matter how polished the figures may be.

Isn't this going to result in a dull dance? Won't the follower get bored? That depends on what you and your partner are looking for. Some leaders manage to fit their entire vocabulary in a single composition to impress or entertain their partner. Sometimes it works, and that's wonderful.

My own preference, though, is to prioritize musicality — especially the way it can deepen the connection between me and my partner. For me, the depth of connection matters more than the breadth of my repertoire. Just as deeper meaning in speech is often expressed with simple words, deeper sense and emotion in dance is often expressed with simple steps.

Of course, walking forward won't get you very far on a crowded dance floor. This is where turns come in. By adding rotation to simple steps, you create a spiral.

> **WALKING IN A TIGHT CIRCLE EXERCISE**
>
> Practice your walk with your partner. Start by walking in a circle to the left (leaders), paying close attention to your form and technique.

> With each step, stretch your main spirals. Exaggerate the turn to make the circle as small as possible — see if you can walk almost on the spot. Then challenge yourself by repeating the exercise while turning to the right.

Dancing the spirals of the phrases is the heart of musicality. Doing this allows you and your partner to truly embody the geometry of the music. You can choose when to open or close the spiral, or when to reverse its direction. The main idea is that you're dancing a specific phrase — you're winding and unwinding its spiral.

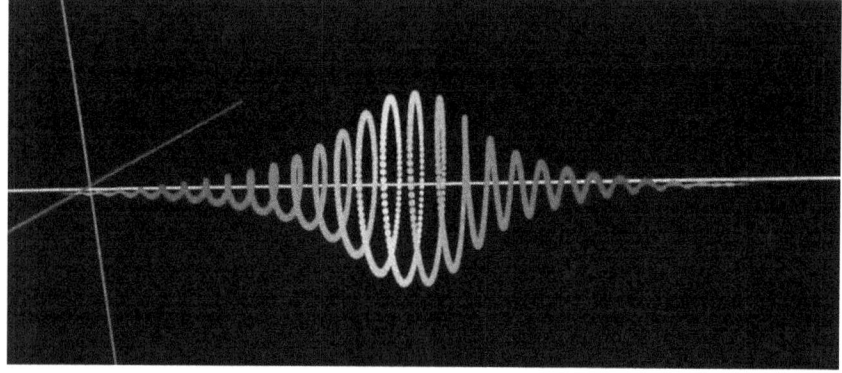

If we look closely at the geometry of tango music, we see that it resembles a structure we've already touched on: a nested spiral, a self-similar fractal helix. Earlier, we explored the spiral nature of sound itself, but how does *music* become a spiral? One way to visualize it is to imagine an octave — a repeating set of twelve notes — as a single turn of the spiral. From this perspective, the piano keyboard, with just over seven octaves, can be "coiled" into seven turns, forming a spiral that runs from the lowest key to the highest.

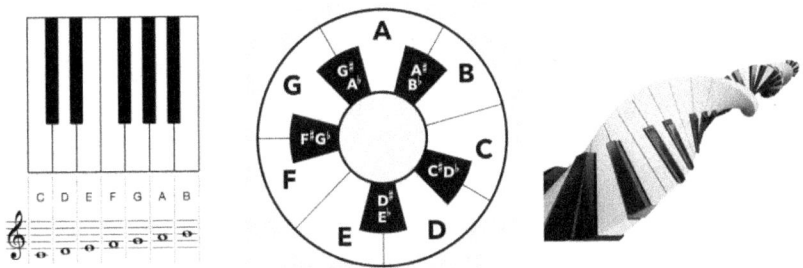

Notes and octaves, however, are rarely played in succession. One theory that describes the structure of tonality as a three-dimensional helix is the Spiral Array Model[38]. A simpler way to visualize the winding nature of music is with the Circle of Fifths, which arranges the primary chords for all major and minor keys in a circular pattern.

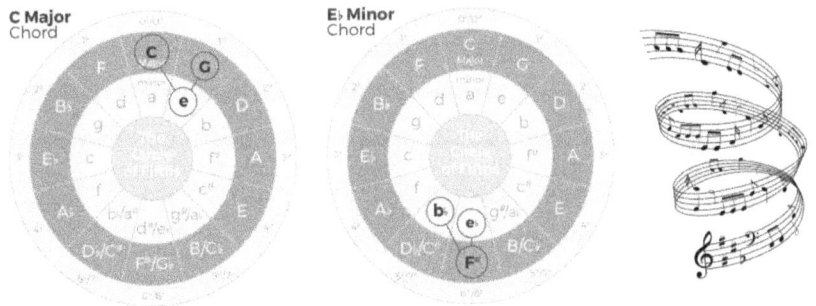

The turns of individual notes, chords, and simple progressions are wound into a larger turn that resembles a phrase. The turns of the phrases then link together to form the spiral of an entire composition.

---

[38] Chew, E. T. THE SPIRAL ARRAY: AN ALGORITHMIC MODEL FOR TONAL SENSORY ORGANIZATION. *Proceedings of the International Conference on Music Perception and Cognition*, 2002.

An opening spiral carries the energy of expansion: reaching out, inhaling, beginning, and growth. A closing spiral carries the energy of contraction: exhaling, conclusion, and protection.

To dance the spiral of a phrase, try picturing its shape. Does the phrase launch with full force, or does it slowly develop from a whisper? In other words, does this sentence begin with ALLCAPS, or is the first word not even capitalized? Does the spiral open or close in the end? In other words, does it end with a definitive period, or does it trail off with an ellipsis? Does this phrase build tension and tighten its winding, or does its energy fade and unwind?

The answers to these questions can help you choose specific combinations of steps and figures that truly express the music. If the spiral of the phrase opens at the end, it may feel natural to finish a giro with a voleo or a *planeo*[39]. If the spiral of the phrase closes, then — depending on the intensity of that close — the giro can end with a simple step to collect, or with a milonguero dip, where the downward closing energy rebounds afterward into the follower's voleo.

Consider how you learn a new language. At first, you translate every word in your head. Then you begin to recognize and adopt phrases. Over time, you get comfortable with your vocabulary. Eventually, you stop focusing on the individual words and instead pay attention to meaning, context, and the essence of the conversation. You learn a language not only to understand others, but also to express your unique perspective.

---

[39] A slow, sweeping circular movement with the foot tracing on the floor.

The same process unfolds in tango. At first, you concentrate on each movement, but as you progress, the steps and figures become second nature. What you've learned becomes part of your body on the level of muscle memory. At that point, your focus may shift to the meaning, context, and the essence of your dance. What you're truly seeking is the bliss of understanding your partner through the embrace, and the bliss of your unique self-expression.

Simplify

The language metaphor works well when it comes to the choice of movement in social tango. When I have a conversation, I don't use most of the complicated words I know. I use such words rarely, only when they're fitting and useful. These moments are sparse — like a semicolon that appears only about once in a chapter.

The same applies to complex figures in dance. Think of them as a pinch of spices in a dish you're cooking. They can certainly enhance the flavor, but too much spices can ruin the whole dish. Five percent? Ten percent? Fine. But 80 percent? There's the garbage bin.

> *"The less you do, the more tango it is."*
> —Dany Flaco

If your usual program consists of running through your entire repertoire of complex figures, there's a good chance it takes away from the finer aspects of your dance: the texture of your movements, the feeling of your partner's touch, the qualities of your embrace, and so on. These subtleties require intention, awareness, and sensitivity, which can only be cultivated through simpler movement. Simplification may feel anticlimactic at first, but it's the right direction if you're seeking bliss within the couple.

> **SIMPLIFY YOUR DANCE EXERCISE**
>
> Pick a familiar tango composition and dance to it with your partner using only forward steps for leaders and back steps for followers. Focus on the quality of each step. To make your dance musical, vary these qualities. Savor each movement. Pause when the music pauses, don't take any steps when the orchestra is quiet. See if you can enjoy the synchronized movement in its simplicity. That joy is the direction we are looking for.

Here's an idea that can both simplify your dance and make it more interesting. If you and your partner are evenly out of phase with each other, then the two of you as a couple move in double time. No complex figures are needed — only simple steps. There's no need to rush or chase the music. In fact, this approach requires one partner to be strategically "lazy," stepping half a beat late. In other words, you and your partner take turns with your steps. By intentionally being half-way out of sync with your partner, you open the door to play, dialogue, and a deeper connection.

Tango music offers plenty of material to explore with your partner without requiring any figures at all. Take syncopation[40], for example

---

[40] Describes a rhythmic pattern that emphasizes the weak beats or off-beats instead of the regular strong beats.

— by simply changing which beat gets the step, you add a new dimension to your dance.

> **FEEL THE SYNCOPATION EXERCISE**
>
> Take a seat and play *Unión Cívica* by Rodolfo Biagi. With your right hand, mark the rhythm of the composition by tapping your thigh, counting "1 2 3 4" as you go. Now hold your left hand above your right — about 20 centimeters above your thigh — and keep it there, letting your right hand come up to meet the left between each tap on your thigh. Your counting now becomes "1 & 2 & 3 & 4 &" — each "&" marking the moment your hands meet. Notice how some of the accents in this composition are syncopated — they fall precisely on this "&."

Not all syncopation is created equal — some syncopation, instead of catching you off guard between beats, falls on beats that aren't usually accented. While most tango compositions emphasize the 1st and 3rd beats, some syncopated accents — especially in Biagi's tangos — fall on the 2nd or 4th.

> **STEP ON THE "2" AND "4" EXERCISE**
>
> Walk with your partner to *Didí* by Rodolfo Biagi (1941) with one limitation: step only on the 2nd and 4th beats. Fortunately, this composition accents many of these "2" and "4" beats. To challenge yourself, try doing the same with Biagi's *Bélgica* (1942). At first, leaders may want to use only forward steps. Once you feel comfortable with syncopation, begin incorporating other steps and figures as well.

The 6th Instrument

The classic Argentine tango orchestra has five instruments: contrabass, piano, violin, bandoneón, and vocals. We can think of the dancing couple as the sixth instrument, since dancers have much in common with the musicians.

A musical composition is in itself a complete work of art — a product of self-expression, to which we can listen. Dance takes that composition further, extending it into the realm of connection, interaction, movement, and play. It becomes a sensory experience that goes beyond listening. Like musicians, the dancing couple expresses the composer's ideas, except not through sound, but through movement.

Another aspect of this analogy is the synergy and coherence among all the instruments in the orchestra. The idea is to be "together," to be part of the transmission, to be on the same wave with the other musicians to such a degree that you become part of that wave. The term *collective improvisation* — which emerged during the jazz era — describes this phenomenon of spontaneity and collaboration, where the entire band improvises together. True collective improvisation is exactly this "riding of the same wave together," where not only is everyone on time, but each musician also seems to somehow know what's coming up next. Since social tango is always improvised, it's fair to say that both leader and follower take part in this kind of collective improvisation.

If there were a conductor, you could imagine her directing both the orchestra and the dancers. The motions of the conductor's hands serve primarily as cues, keeping all the musicians together. Another way to see it is that the dancing couple *is* the conductor. This sometimes happens at milongas when people are dancing to a live orchestra — the musicians themselves may take their cues from the dancers.

Live Music

I will never forget one afternoon dancing to a live orchestra in Barcelona. The milonga was held outdoors in a beautiful park. There was plenty of space, good traffic, and the musicians brought out all the richness, dynamics, and emotion of the tango compositions they played. My partner and I were enjoying it so much that we danced through both sets without a break. What surprised us most was that on several occasions our stumbles coincided perfectly with the musicians' slip-ups. It felt as if we were so in tune with the orchestra that even our "mistakes" happened together — and we could hear our missteps echoed in the music.

Dancing to a recording is like riding an unchanging wave. A recorded composition sounds the same every time you play it. Nonetheless, the golden-age recordings are so brilliant that they continue to inspire dancers to this day. Dancing to a live orchestra is like riding a wave as it's being created in the moment. Something larger comes alive: the dancers, in turn, inspire the musicians, who are playing live. We take part in shaping the wave we're riding.

This closes the energy loop, creates resonance, and can lead to extraordinary experiences for everyone involved. A loop like this has the power to amplify joy to a level beyond anything you may have felt before.

The image that resonates most with me is that the music comes from within the couple, not from outside. Just like the other instruments, the music flows from our bodies and is expressed through movement. The difference is that, unlike acoustic instruments, our bodies are "movement instruments." Dancing to a live orchestra in Barcelona, we weren't just on the same wavelength with the musicians — we were *one* with them. It felt much like the bliss of playing live in a tight-knit, well-coordinated music band. As any musician will tell you, that feeling of euphoria is why they do what they do.

Each time we dance, even to a recording, our dance is unique. The magic of dancing to a live tango orchestra is that the uniqueness goes even further — this musical moment will never be repeated. Even if the same orchestra plays the same composition again, it will sound a little different. That fleeting quality, the sense of sharing something absolutely unique, makes you feel fortunate and grateful, adding tremendously to your bliss.

Abstractions

In my tango adolescence, I took a group class that left a lasting impression on me. At that stage, I hadn't yet discovered the variety of tango music — I simply didn't have the experience. In beginner and intermediate group lessons, teachers often play easy (read "boring") compositions. But in this class, the teacher introduced us to the Elements in tango music: *air*, *water*, *earth*, and *fire*. We danced to two compositions for each element. I'm fairly sure *air* was Osvaldo Fresedo, another orchestra for *water*, *earth*, of course, was Juan D'Arienzo. The last one — Osvaldo Pugliese — ignited something primal in me, a fire that has been burning ever since.

When you categorize tango music into archetypes, when you begin to feel the essence of each composition, something liberating happens. You stop dancing the rhythm. You stop dancing the figures. Instead, you begin to dance the mood, the energy, the abstraction. This shift is liberating, because it leads you away from constraints and toward the state you're truly seeking.

Our brains can assign color to music, depending on how a composition makes us feel. If I were to DJ, I would assign each piece its own palette of hues — from beginning to end — and then select tandas visually. This is one kind of abstraction you might enjoy exploring. Does the music feel ice-cold or burning hot? Do you feel it deep in your gut or on the surface of your skin? Where does it take you? What taste does it leave in your mouth? If you notice that sound connects naturally for you with another sense, explore that connection — it may unlock new dimensions of your musicality.

Another way to develop musicality is to focus on the context of the music. What is this composition about? You don't need to understand Spanish to sense the answer — many compositions are instrumental anyway. Instead, feel for the answer. Let your emotions guide you, and focus on what the music stirs in you. Zoom out from this musical moment and look for the bigger picture: what was the composer trying to say with the piece as a whole?

> **FOCUS ON THE MUSIC EXERCISE**
>
> Dance with your partner to a lesser-known composition with one additional challenge: lower the volume until you can barely hear it. At first this may feel uncomfortable, but it will sharpen your focus and draw your full attention to the music. Remember to breathe. If

> you lose track of the music, stop moving — don't try to guess or fill in the gaps. Simply wait, and continue dancing when you hear it again.

Unspoken Agreements

There is a kind of unspoken agreement between tango dancers and tango music composers. This agreement has to do with the structure of the music. I don't just mean the typical format of tango compositions, which consists of phrases of the same length. I'm referring to the subtler patterns and repetitions that appear in nearly all popular tangos: a syncopation that recurs in every phrase, alternating staccato and *legato*[41] passages, or a particular accent at the end of every other phrase. There are tons of examples.

Of course, there are rare exceptions and playful "gotcha" moments. But for the most part, this agreement is there to make tango music easy to dance to. When you look for this "hidden" structure, the patterns and repetitions reveal themselves. You begin to sense exactly what musical moment is coming next — even when you're dancing to a piece you've never heard before.

Another unspoken agreement in tango music pertains to the transitions between contrasting parts of a composition. Like the unspoken agreement above, it exists to support your improvisation on the social dance floor.

---

[41] A style of playing music in which the notes are smoothly connected, with no perceptible breaks between them.

To signal that a change is coming, musicians often use *foreshadowing*. One or two beats before the change takes place, they begin to prepare the dancers. The orchestra may build toward a crescendo, soften into a decrescendo, or let one instrument introduce the next part slightly ahead of time. These cues, aside from sounding exquisite, are there to guide you. They let you know what is about to unfold.

Like a helpful prompter, tango music itself tells you what's coming up next. To take advantage of this, all you need to do is trust the musicians and stay fully present with what the music is offering in the moment.

Tango music is always on your side. These masterpieces were written and recorded to help you not only dance well, but also thoroughly enjoy your every step. Musicality in tango is a clear path to absolute bliss.

Stability and Technique

In tango lessons, teachers often use the word *balance* to describe the importance of each partner's individual stability within the couple. Technically, balance means two or more forces brought into equilibrium. The idea conjures up images of the ancient hanging scales held by blindfolded Justice. But is balance really the right term for tango technique?

To take a step, we must go out of balance. In dance, balance is fleeting — we are truly balanced only for a brief moment. So balance is not the ultimate goal of tango technique. What we are really seeking is *stability*: controlled cycles of moving in and out of balance while remaining stable.

Personal stability is the cornerstone of all tango technique. When my partner and I are stable, the foundation is there — we are dancing, and we can begin to explore the next levels of our priorities pyramid. Without personal stability, tango turns into partner management, with one person constantly putting out localized imbalance "fires" one after another. Forget bliss — we're doing our best to remain upright.

What makes personal stability so challenging is that in tango we have to be stable while standing on one foot. This is perhaps the most technically demanding part of the dance. The good news is that stability has several components, each of which can be understood, practiced, and improved.

Stability begins with grounding. Imagine four points on the sole of your foot that you can engage to anchor yourself properly. Leaders can press down on all four of these points with equal pressure to create a stable base for their structure. You might picture your foot fastened to the floor with screws at those points, or imagine four roots growing down into the floor.

Followers can also use these four points as a grounding image, with one key difference. In followers' technique — especially when wearing heels — more weight is placed on the ball of the foot, and never entirely on the heel.

A properly engaged foot shortens slightly and curls inward. The anatomy behind this is fascinating, but for our purposes it's enough to know this: your foot is well engaged when you feel a muscle working along the outer side of your shin, just below the knee.

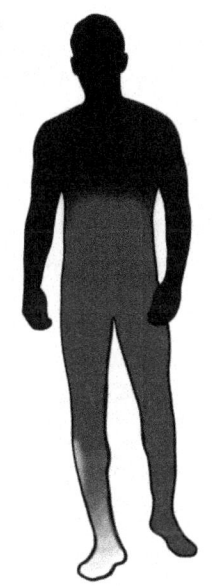

If you stand on one foot and pay close attention, you'll notice that most of the adjustments keeping you steady happen in your ankle. To get a clearer picture, you can imagine a "heat map" of muscular engagement in tango: white and light gray show maximal engagement, while dark gray and black show minimal engagement.

PUT ON YOUR SHOES WHILE STANDING ON ONE FOOT EXERCISE

It's best to turn this exercise into a **daily habit** for training your stability. When tying or untying your shoes, or when putting them on or taking them off, avoid sitting or coming down to the floor. Instead, stand on one foot and lift the other by raising your knee, bringing your foot up to your hands. Keep your back straight. The few seconds it takes to sort out your shoes are enough to engage the standing foot and reinforce the feeling of stability. Small actions you repeat every day shape your physiology and condition you, steadily contributing to your improvement.

To ground yourself, you need to send your center of mass downward, as low as possible. Your body allows this because it isn't solid or made of a single material. You can shift your center of mass by imagining a point where all your weight is concentrated, then visualizing that point moving down toward your knees. If you hold this image in your mind while dancing, your movements will naturally reflect a lowered center of mass.

Another key aspect of stability and technique is your axis. The idea is to stretch your axis in two directions: downward, by pushing the floor with your standing foot, and upward, by expanding through your spine. When these two opposing vectors are properly engaged, they form a solid structure of your axis.

Maintaining your axis allows you to stay connected in the embrace without being dependent on your partner. A well-formed axis frees you from any need to push, pull, or otherwise use your partner for stability. These opposing vectors are especially important in out-of-axis figures such as *colgadas*[42] and *volcadas*[43] — the upward vector is what allows you to feel light for your partner, even when you intentionally lean your axis.

If you lean your axis onto your partner without stretching upward, you will be heavy to dance with. This creates the effect of pushing down on your partner and makes them responsible for holding you up.

It's also important never to lean your axis onto your partner through your head. The forehead is the hardest part of the human

---

[42] Off-axis move where dancers lean away from each other, sharing counterbalance.
[43] Off-axis move where the partners lean into each other.

body, and if you force it against any part of your partner's body, it can cause discomfort or even pain. Of course, a gentle contact with your partner's head can feel nice. This is a personal choice and something to be negotiated within the uniqueness of your couple's embrace. Personally, I like having the option to go either way. For example, I like to keep a soft, comfortable head contact when lyrical music inspires more hugging and less movement, and no head contact at all when the music is passionate and dynamic.

How do you maintain your axis in the dance? The key is to dissociate *around* it without moving, breaking, or changing the orientation of your axis.

> ### Dissociation Pivots Exercise
>
> Stand up straight and choose the foot you'll pivot on — this will also set the direction of your pivot. Begin by dissociating your upper body in that direction without moving your pelvis. This first step "winds the spring." When you reach the natural limit of your dissociation, hold your upper body in place and pivot in the same direction, bringing your pelvis into alignment. This second step "unwinds the spring." It helps to *exhale* during this part. Be careful not to rely on the momentum of your upper body to complete the pivot. Keep your body and head upright so nothing throws you off balance.
>
> Once you feel comfortable with this two-part pivot in both directions, you can expand its range by adding a third part. Instead of simply aligning your pelvis to your upper body in the second step, go a little further — "over-associate" — so your pelvis dissociates even more in the same direction. Then, add a third step, bringing your upper body into alignment with your lower body. This over-

> association, followed by the third step of the exercise, naturally extends the range of your pivot.

To maintain the integrity of your axis, the muscles of your core have to be engaged. This includes your back, obliques, abs, and psoas. The key is for these muscle groups to work evenly, each contributing its share to support your axis. If, for example, you relax your abs while overworking your back to compensate, your axis might feel stable while you're associated. But as soon as you turn or dissociate, this compensatory mechanism will break your axis and throw both you and your partner off balance.

When dancing tango, the engagement of your core should be roughly ten percent of a plank. Of course, a plank is static, while tango is dynamic, but this image gives you a sense of the engagement usually needed when dancing. On the one hand, it may not sound exciting to think of tango as exercise. On the other hand, what better way to train your body than while embracing someone?

There are many exercises that can strengthen and condition your core, though they are beyond the scope of this book. What matters here is understanding that your core is the central pillar of your axis, and engaging it is essential to your technique.

When you internalize the concepts described above, your axis becomes sturdy while still allowing you to freely dissociate. This is more than enough for most figures in social dancing. But if you wish, you can delve deeper into this subject.

One of my recent partners, for example, loves to play with her axis. She deliberately curves it during out-of-axis figures while fully maintaining its integrity. Her axis is like a steel rod that has been gently bowed. This tanguera is quite petite, and by bending her axis during figures like volcadas, she adds mass to the dynamics of her movement. Playing with mass "created" in this way adds a whole new dimension to the dance. She can adjust her movement dynamics during turns in response to the music — choosing to stay light, or to curve her axis and become massive. She can use it to slow us down, and to generate centripetal force in rotation.

This tanguera doesn't become heavy — there's a difference. She isn't placing her *weight* on me. Instead, she creates *mass*, the three-dimensional movement dynamics of which can vary. The distinction between weight and mass is simple: the vector of weight is always downward, while mass is what resists acceleration or deceleration, regardless of direction.

There are no straight lines in nature. Our axis in tango, though an imaginary construct, can also curve slightly, and this can add to your stability. Spirals are holographic — any segment of a spiral contains the information about the whole. A subtle curve in the axis is a small piece of the larger spiral, and this can be explored in the dance. Out-of-axis figures invite you to play with the curve of your axis, revealing its spiral nature. Ask an architect, and she will confirm that a spiral structure is more stable than one built using straight lines. In the same way, exploring this approach in tango can reveal new potential for better stability.

Our Two Main Spirals

For our purposes, the two main spirals in your body form an "X." One spans from your left shoulder to the toes of your right foot, and the other from your right shoulder to the toes of your left foot. Expanding one spiral while contracting the other is what allows you to dissociate while staying on the same vertical level.

This idea requires that you activate the entire spiral each time you extend it: spine, pelvis, hip, knee, ankle, foot, and toes. I recently danced with a petite tanguera and noticed something very peculiar. Dancing with her prompted me to engage my toes with every step. This sensation was so distinct that I couldn't help but notice and "lean into it." Perhaps because of her small form, she was engaging the entirety of her spirals, right down to her toes. I could actually feel how her toes contributed to the precision of her steps. I tend to mirror the subtle qualities of my partner's movements, so that tanda became an inward exploration and learning about the capabilities within my own body.

To understand how much work each part of a spiral should contribute, consider the length of each segment. Nature tends to design our bodies in a way that size relates to function, and you'll notice this proportionality when comparing different segments of your spirals. In other words, the effort of each segment in the spiral should be roughly proportional to its size in relation to the others.

If a part of your spiral is blocked — if one of the joints isn't participating in extending and contracting — this throws a wrench in the entire concept. This can mean one of two things: either your spirals do not fully extend and contract, or the other segments must overwork to compensate. This forces your body to engage compensatory mechanisms, which results in several problems. First, compensation requires more effort than natural movement, leading to tension and strain. Second, compensatory mechanisms don't feel, look, or perform as well as natural movements.

When I first started learning tango, I realized I wasn't engaging my feet. With practice, I began to notice the difference between "stepping onto my foot" and "engaging my whole foot throughout the entire step." This meant paying attention to every stage: touchdown, compression, arrival, preparation, decompression, and departure. It also meant actively rolling through the entire foot. I'm still learning how to fully engage my spirals with each step.

Gravity

To dance tango, it actually takes three. Without the Earth and her gravity, we wouldn't even be able to take a single step. Our embrace with the Earth, the way she continually pulls us in, is what makes it possible for my partner and me to communicate with each other in the embrace.

The phrase "push the floor," which my tango teachers repeated again and again, didn't make much sense to me at first. It went in one ear and out the other. I remember thinking, I'm already doing so much — why would I add extra effort by pushing the floor if I'm already resisting gravity?

The answer is that pushing the floor is the key to communication in tango. When I press into the floor with my standing foot, I engage my axis and expand my main spiral. It's one of the main ways we communicate in the embrace. This tells my partner not only which leg I'm standing on, but also where I am, what I'm doing with my body, and where I'm going next. By pushing the floor, I organize my body so that the energy of that push moves upward, through my axis, and toward my partner.

Consider an ancient stone arch bridge, with both sides firmly rooted in bedrock. Each side rises, stone by stone, until the two arches meet at the center. This is the essence of pushing the floor — creating an arch of energy that meets in the embrace.

Of course, this picture is incomplete, because a bridge is static. In tango, pushing the floor allows you to *vary* how much energy you send upward into the embrace. This variation, in turn, allows your partner to match this energy by expanding and contracting their spirals. Once you discover the potential in this variability, there is no going back. Gravity becomes your trusted ally — it's the foundation on which you can build a clear line of communication with your partner.

Being Light or Massive

Some of the more nuanced moments in tango may call for you to feel lighter or more massive to your partner. Your weight doesn't change during the dance — so how is this possible?

The key is perception. What your partner feels has little to do with your actual measurements. Acrobats and gymnasts have a technique that allows them to be perceived as light to their partners, who throw them into the air and catch them. The performer being lifted or thrown thinks "up" and imagines herself as a bird about to take flight.

This mental image prompts her to engage her core and create just the right amount of tone in her muscles. The athlete collects and groups her body, creating the perfect form for the task. These changes in her physical organization are what makes her feel light to her partners.

What's the right amount of tone? Think of it as similar to the "ten percent of a plank" reference for engaging your core. In the following graph, the far left shows the "Dead Weight" point, where there is no tone at all and your weight simply hangs on your bones. This is when your body feels the heaviest.

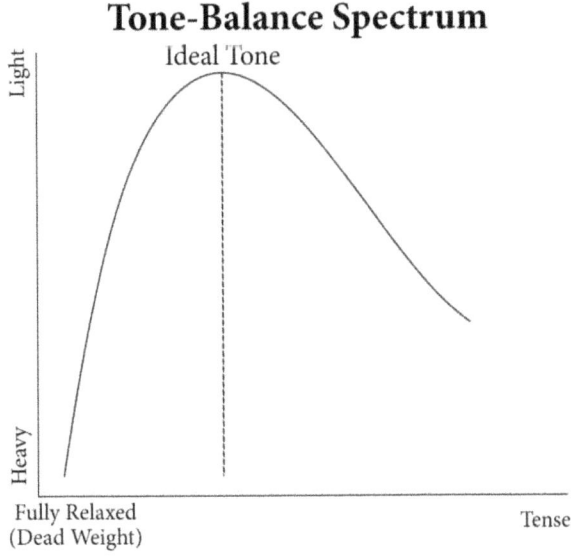

The lightest "Ideal Tone" point is reached quite quickly. But then something interesting happens: as you add more and more tension, you actually start to feel heavy again. Since we don't want tension in our dance, we'll focus only on the left side of this graph, where lightness comes from finding just enough tone.

There are moments in dance when we may actually want parts of ourselves to feel more massive. In social tango these are rare, but they do exist (think Osvaldo Pugliese's *Pasional*). For example, during a planeo the follower might want her free leg to be perceived as massive.

To create this effect, the follower can intensify the figure's counterforce vector, which we discussed in *Controlled Movement*. This means increasing her body tone in opposition to the rotational direction. If, on the other hand, she reduces the counterforce vector, the leader will perceive her free leg as light.

In the end, whether you feel light or massive comes down to the amount of tone in your muscles, which you can vary using abstraction and visualization.

Light or Massive Exercise

Dance to a slow composition that allows the follower to occasionally change her muscle tone — breathing "up" and making herself light, then shifting to being heavy, and then returning to being light again. The leader's task is to notice these changes and describe them to the follower in real time, including where the "mass" is located. Throughout the composition, lead several planeos. The follower can make her free leg feel either heavy or light, and the leader's task is to sense and distinguish the difference.

Improvement

For many of us, learning to dance means noticing the patterns that don't work, unlearning them, and replacing them with something that works. This isn't always straightforward. What can help with this process?

The first step — unlearning, or letting go of what no longer serves you — doesn't require extra effort. In fact, unlearning is more about letting go. One of the biggest reasons people resist change is an unconscious fear of the unknown "new," which makes them cling to the familiar "old" way of doing things.

Next time you struggle with an exercise in class, try asking yourself, *What am I afraid of?* I remember one moment when this question revealed to me that I was afraid of stepping on my partner's toes. That awareness, followed by reassurance that my fear was unjustified, was what allowed the exercise to finally click for me.

Two keys to improvement are believing that progress is possible and truly wanting it. When you want to improve, you also want to understand exactly *what* needs attention. A good way to discover this is by asking your dance partners for feedback.

You may not notice your own habits, but they can be very clear to the people you dance with. While it goes against *códigos*[44] to teach on the dance floor at a milonga, there are plenty of other opportunities to receive feedback. *When you ask them*, sensitive partners will often give you valuable insights.

Of course, not all feedback will be about you, useful, accurate, or even true. Here are some ways to recognize discardable feedback in tango. First — if you didn't ask for feedback to begin with. Second — if it makes you feel bad: judgments, passive-aggressive remarks, unsolicited psychoanalysis, assessments of your form or character, and so on. Third — if it stands alone as an outlier that doesn't match what you consistently hear from other partners.

If you approach this process with curiosity, much like a scientist collecting data, and listen to several partners, you'll start to see a complete picture of what you need to work on. This will help you set goals and move toward them. Keep in mind that as you progress, your goals will change. In other words, never stop asking for feedback, and continue to learn. Stay flexible, embrace change as the only constant, and guide it in the direction of your goals.

During the early years of my tango journey, after about a year and a half of lessons, I went to learn in Buenos Aires. At one particularly crowded milonga, I witnessed a stunning performance. The performing couple looked very young — perhaps only 18 years old. They danced with unbelievable skill — their technique was impeccable, their dance was filled with emotions and brimming with life. The audience gave them a standing ovation.

---

[44] Unwritten rules of behavior at tango events, such as floor etiquette, communication, and invitation customs.

The next day, I attended a group lesson at a place I hadn't visited before, and what I saw there astonished me. Among the beginners, learning to walk and paying attention to the instructor, was the very same young man who had received a standing ovation the night before. At first, I couldn't believe my eyes. I walked up to him and asked, "Excuse me, were you the one performing last night?" He smiled, shook my hand, and introduced himself: "Krishna."

My shock turned into a profound insight. This young dancer understood something essential. Instead of resting on his laurels or training only to maintain his form, he knew there was always more to learn — something new to discover. Even in the most basic lesson, where they teach you how to walk.

If you're not actively looking for ways to improve, your progress will only happen "by accident" — for example, if the topic of a group class happens to match what you need, or if your teacher points it out. This leads to an important question: how do you find a tango teacher, who is right for you? In my experience, three major factors make a good tango teacher.

Character. This is a big one. Beyond learning to dance, we pick up a myriad of quirks and traits from a teacher — whether we want to or not. This is true of anyone we grant authority to, especially when we spend significant time with them and follow their guidance. Over time, a teacher's personality begins to rub off on us, and we inevitably become a little like them. So it's worth asking: is this a good person? Are they kind, respectful, and considerate of others, both on and off the dance floor?

Teachers hold a great deal of power, and with that comes responsibility. Unfortunately, some tango teachers are addicts, narcissists, manipulators, and so on. They are human, like everyone else, and the title of "tango teacher" does not automatically absolve anyone of character flaws. The real question is: how do they use their influence? Do they use it for personal gain, or do their words and, more importantly, their actions unite your tango community? Do they include or ostracize people? Do they build bridges, or do they constantly quarrel with other teachers and organizers? In other words, is this someone you want as a role model?

What drives this person? Is this teacher genuinely interested in your progress, or do they keep you running in circles, making you come back to them, because they are corrupted by money, admiration or power? A good teacher has your best interests at heart and wants to see you grow above all else. Is their true motivation contribution, or self-aggrandizement? A person's real character often shows in challenging social situations. Be observant, trust your instincts, use your judgment, and don't let anyone take advantage of you.

Skills. Does this teacher have what you need? Before deciding whether a particular teacher has skills, I suggest getting clear on what you're looking for. Perhaps your main focus is how the dance feels within the couple. Or maybe you want to explore and develop your body's natural movement dynamics. Your objectives may vary, and they can change over time. Each goal requires a different skill set — and not every tango teacher will have what you need.

There's no universal "litmus test" for skills in tango. A championship prize might suggest that someone is highly skilled, but if you think about it, such awards are based only on how their tango *looks*. I doubt anyone has ever received a prize for the most melting embrace. And of course, many excellent dancers never compete at all. To decide whether a teacher has the skills you want to develop, I recommend paying attention to how they dance, dancing with them if you get the chance, and — if possible — talking to and dancing with their students.

One important aside: dancing with a potential teacher should feel good. If it doesn't, it may be because they aren't the right teacher for you, or because they're using the following trick. Sadly, some teachers resort to recruiting their students by making them feel bad on the dance floor. They might invite you to dance at a milonga and leave you feeling incompetent, so that you believe they are skilled and turn to them for improvement. A good teacher will always adapt their dance to meet you where you are. This always feels good, and it's the only true starting point for growth.

Pedagogy. Can this person give you what you're looking for? Having a skill does not automatically mean someone can teach it; there are many great dancers who are not strong teachers. Pedagogy is a skill of its own, and beyond love for the craft, it requires both the desire and the ability to transfer knowledge to the student. A good teacher can personalize their approach and adapt to the way each student learns. Do you learn best by visualizing an exercise in your mind, by watching it performed, or by feeling it in your own body? A good teacher will recognize and use the method that works best for you.

> *"When the student is ready the teacher will appear. When the student is truly ready... The teacher will disappear."*
> —Tao Te Ching

I also recommend switching to a different teacher after a while — or at least trying classes with other teachers, including visiting maestras — and here's why. You may learn something entirely new, or suddenly "get" something that hadn't been working for you before. Even if you encounter conflicting viewpoints, you'll be able to choose the perspective that serves you best. Some teachers work better with beginners, others with advanced students, and over time you'll start to recognize the difference. Don't be afraid of hurting your teacher's feelings by learning from someone else. A good teacher's main goal is your progress, and the way you choose to improve is always your personal decision.

Finding the right tango teacher can be especially challenging in a small community, but I assure you this person exists. You may even turn out to be their very first student. Take your time, stay open to opportunities, and trust your instincts. If you keep these factors in mind, you will find the teacher who is right for you — whether you've been dancing for five days or five years.

My encounter with Krishna in a beginners' class gave me a profound insight: learning is a never-ending process. I keep learning because I don't see a final destination on this path. I can't imagine a moment when I would declare the process complete. I attend classes not only to teach my body something new, but also to further free myself and allow my body to truly dance.

At the same time, I'm not chasing perfection. In fact, I would argue that perfection — always just on the horizon — points in the opposite direction of bliss. Perfection is the aim of the extrinsically motivated; bliss is an intrinsic reward. You can certainly discover beauty in the search for bliss, but if you insist on perfection, euphoria will continue to elude you. My practice partner recently reflected on my attitude toward "misunderstandings" in our dance: "It's such a relief — some of my other partners stress when something goes wrong, but those moments don't seem to bother you at all." More often than not, we simply laugh when something like that happens.

A famous maestro admitted in an interview that every new figure they came up with was the result of a "mistake" made during practice. But were they really mistakes, if their attitude transformed them into discoveries?

Nobody's perfect. We all have quirks, weird habits, and silly things we do, all of which are unique to our individual expression. If you view them not as annoyances to eradicate, but as facets of your personality, you liberate a significant portion of your psycho-emotional resources. If your imperfections don't stand in the way of your dancing, if they're not hurting you, your partner, or other couples around you, then they're simply a part of your character, a part of who you are.

When you're not chasing perfection, when you let go of the high bar of expectations, and stop comparing yourself to others, you become free. Allow yourself to make mistakes, laugh about the moments of indecision. Remember, it's just a dance — the social dance floor is the last place where you want to feel stressed.

Style

Your dance and your style are always unique. You don't even need to worry about that — it will always be true. Categorizations, labels, exclusions, and definitions only box you in and limit your self-expression. Give yourself the freedom to decide whether you even want to categorize your dance style at all. That freedom is what allows your individuality to flourish. Take what you love from each style you encounter and make it part of your vocabulary, make it your own. Leave the rest, like at a buffet.

> *"Mastery is not about perfection. It's about a process, a journey."*
> —George Leonard

Embrace change. Train your body to adapt continuously, and celebrate each time you notice something new beginning to emerge. Don't stress over the low points on your progress graph — see all change as a positive indicator of your growth. Allow this constant evolution to become the fertile ground where your unique style of tango can take root and blossom. The character and style of your dance are the dynamic expression of your individuality. Your style is ultimately defined by the degree of openness and freedom you allow yourself to express.

This may be a personal quirk, but I feel a spark of euphoria every time something *new* comes through in my dance. Sometimes it's a long-forgotten figure I once learned but never made part of my vocabulary, a new sequence, or even a new way of being out of phase with my partner. Each moment of novelty is my personal mini bliss. Look for similar gems in your own experience. Discover what makes your heart do cartwheels, and dive into it fully. Your style — and your personal sources of joy — are always yours to choose.

All great artists, regardless of their medium, have acknowledged that their masterpieces are not their own. A true masterpiece can only come *through* the artist once they understand that they are a conduit — a channel merely assisting the art in its emerging. It's a paradox: the sooner you disidentify from your tango, get out of your own way, and allow the dance to come through your unique prism of self-expression, the sooner your tango becomes a genuine art form that is unmistakably yours. When you let go of ideas like "my tango," "my performance," and "my style," you free yourself from pressure, self-criticism, and control. That freedom creates a clear path to your authentic self-expression — and walking that path feels like pure bliss.

Psychology

I recently came across the results of a psychological study that left me puzzled. The researchers claimed that our level of happiness is determined by a mix of circumstances, genetics, and psychology. They even assigned percentage points to each factor: between 30% and 40% of our happiness, they said, comes from our genes, with the rest divided between psychology and circumstances.

What puzzled me is that I believe our psychology alone is responsible for our overall happiness. My bold claim is based on the idea that psychology influences both our circumstances and our genes. Scientists have shown that our genes change[45] throughout our lives, and research from the HeartMath Institute suggests that human emotions can directly affect DNA structure[46]. In other words, our habitual psychological state plays a major role in shaping our genetic expression. As for circumstances, even the most skeptical materialist would have to admit that our psychology directly affects our

---

[45] Manders, F.; van Boxtel, R.; Middelkamp, S. The Dynamics of Somatic Mutagenesis During Life in Humans. Frontiers in Aging Genetics, 2022.
[46] McCraty, R., Atkinson, M., Tomasino, D., & Bradley, R. T. (2003). Modulation of DNA conformation by heart-focused intention. Boulder Creek, CA: HeartMath Research Center, Institute of HeartMath. Publication No. 03-008.

circumstances and our environment. Put simply, our mindset determines whether we accept and leave things as they are, change our situation, or remove ourselves from it altogether.

The foundation of our psychology is our worldview: the way we see ourselves, other people, and the world in general. Do I feel helpless at the mercy of fate, or do I believe I am responsible for everything I experience because I create my world from the inside out? Are the people in my life there by chance, or is there a reason for this? Is the world a dangerous or a friendly place? Of course, these are extremes — worldviews are far more complex than simple answers to these questions. Still, it's unlikely that someone with a cynical or pessimistic worldview will generally be happy.

What does bliss have to do with happiness? When you're happy, you're almost there. But if your usual states are despair and contempt, then you have a ways to go. Compare the experiences of an optimist and a pessimist, and you'll notice something fascinating: the pessimist continually sees proof of his pessimism, while the optimist continually sees proof of his optimism. The paradox is that both are right! The real question is, "Is your worldview working out for you?" If it isn't, you can change it. Once you make that decision, the next question becomes, "How do I do that?"

> *"Get happy, and the evidence will present itself."*
> —Abraham Hicks

It's all about perspective — the light in which you see your circumstances, your point of view. Even if you cannot change the situation itself, you always have the power to change how you look at it and the meaning you assign to the situation. Freedom is in having options. We constantly choose the direction of our thoughts, our perspectives, and the meanings we assign to our experience. What's clear is that if you have only one perspective to choose from — only one option — then it's not really a choice, it's a knee-jerk reaction.

When I explain the idea behind this book to fellow tango dancers, they sometimes ask, "But what if people disagree with your suggestions?" My goal is not to prove anything, to challenge anyone, to be right, or to claim some ultimate truth. My goal is simply to offer people who want to change something in themselves a set of additional *perspectives*, so that they may find greater freedom in choosing how they see things the next time an opportunity presents itself.

Beginner's Journey

Nothing will humble you more effectively than the feeling of being a total beginner. We've all been there, and if you're a beginner now — my heart goes out to you. Almost anyone can go to the first class, but to go to a second and third class — to keep at it and move toward your goal even when you're not seeing much progress — that takes courage.

What do you get as an immediate reward? Oh, it's a lovely bouquet of feelings: shame, self-doubt, the desire for approval, the fear of making mistakes, and the desire to fit in and belong to the community. All this can feel like too much — no wonder many people quit after a while. But if you approach these feelings with curiosity, you'll see there's absolutely no reason to get discouraged.

Not everyone is a perfectionist, but we all have a part of our personality that wants to see us as good, skillful, mature, and capable. This part can quickly come into conflict with being a tango beginner who has to learn how to walk (what am I — a child?), producing all those feelings of shame and self-criticism. This inner conflict is simply a matter of perspective. Understand that you can be good, mature, capable — and still be a tango novice. Allow yourself to be an absolute beginner, no matter how long this stage lasts. Just keep going to class.

Everyone at the milonga — maestros included — was a beginner once. No one is judging you — everyone remembers this stage from their own experience and likely had very similar feelings about themselves not too long ago. So the next time you meet an advanced partner's *mirada*[47] — don't hide your eyes. There's no need to wait until you're "good enough." Dance. Allow yourself to make mistakes. Own your beginner's journey, and you won't even notice how quickly you will no longer be a beginner.

Know Thyself

Why do people come to tango? What draws them to this particular social dance, when others have a much easier learning curve and allow you to start dancing socially after the first group lesson? I doubt it's simply the challenge that brings people to tango. More often, I believe that within the complexities of leading, following, and moving together lies a deeper psychological motive — the desire to improve one's relationships.

---

[47] Eye contact used to signal interest in dancing; part of the invitation ritual, a precursor to *cabeceo*.

Many women, for example, come to tango as a way to learn how to trust men again. Physical, sexual, or emotional trauma can leave someone unable to trust men in general. In the dance, the follower has to trust the leader with navigational safety, among other things. The essence of the follower mode — the follower's immediate, reflective responses to the lead — relies on fully trusting the leader's signals. In a way, every step in tango is an affirmation of the follower's trust in the leader. These partner dynamics of social tango can provide women with opportunities to heal and gradually rebuild trust.

I came to tango because I sensed it could become my body practice — a way to train the body that would also condition the mind. For various psychological reasons, our bodies sometimes create blockages that interrupt natural movement. To compensate, we develop movement patterns that look and feel unnatural. These compensatory mechanisms often go unnoticed simply because we grow accustomed to them.

That is, until an observant teacher with a sharp eye points them out. I vividly remember one tango lesson when my teacher identified each of my blockages one by one: the neck, the pelvis, and the feet. With each point, I experienced a mini-revelation. I could clearly sense the psychological root behind every block: unhealthy views of the opposite sex, feeling unsure in my masculinity, lack of stability in my life. In that moment, I realized tango had the potential to help me work on myself and improve my psychology. Later, when I began engaging my pelvis and adjusting my walk to reflect its natural dynamics, my tango improved tremendously. Psychology and physiology are deeply intertwined, and I can say with certainty that my mindset improved as well.

Tango resembles life and relationships in a very interesting way. Social tango is like a magnifying glass: the traits and patterns we may try to hide from ourselves or others inevitably surface in the dance or around the dance floor.

One tanguera mentioned that she cannot maintain long-distance relationships or even long-distance friendships. For her, it was easier to end the relationship and forget — out of sight, out of mind — than to maintain a virtual connection. This tendency revealed itself in her dance as well: she resisted opening the embrace. Off the dance floor, when I pointed out that in an open embrace we're really not that far from each other, we had a good laugh about this.

One leader is never quite sure which direction she wants to take her partner. At times, she seems to wait for the follower to take the initiative before she goes along with the movement. Another leader cannot dance in close embrace — for him it's too intimate, too close. There is nothing inherently wrong with these cases. Social tango simply mirrors our psychology, offering a glimpse into our inner world. Of course, our psychology can be complex beyond our own understanding, which is why I recommend working with a professional, in order to heal.

The desire to look in the mirror of social tango must come from within. The main point is that we always have a choice: to recognize certain qualities in ourselves, decide we want something different, and take specific steps toward change — or continue to do the same.

Mindset

We can consider two main types of mindsets: a fixed mindset and a growth mindset[48]. A fixed mindset resists change, while a growth mindset actively seeks opportunities to reflect, question its own approach, adapt, and grow. At the core of both lies a deeper question of identity — the most profound question we can ask: "Who am I?"

Someone with a fixed mindset identifies closely with their own mind. Their psyche resembles a rigid structure built on a solid foundation of concepts learned early in life[49]. If someone or something challenges the validity of those concepts, the person with a fixed mindset tends to resist and defend their point of view. Beneath this reaction is often an unconscious fear: that if even one of these "bearing walls" is removed, the entire structure will collapse, and they may lose their mind. Rigidity is fragile. When someone identifies with their mind, any challenge to their worldview is perceived as a personal attack.

A person with a growth mindset understands that they are much more than their mind. They see the mind as the best tool at their disposal, and they know that in order to make the best use of it, they must keep it sharp. This means continually refining and adapting it to meet the growing complexities of their experience. Today's fast-paced world, with its exponentially accelerating change, science, and progress, downright demands this approach. A growth mindset

---

[48] Dweck, C., PhD. Mindset: The New Psychology of Success. Ballantine Books, 2007.
[49] Singer, M. The Untethered Soul: The Journey Beyond Yourself. New Harbinger Publications/ Noetic Books, 2007.

carries the true spirit of science — if someone can celebrate being proven wrong, that's a clear sign of a growth mindset.

The greatest challenge in learning tango is that, beyond changing our bodies, we must also be willing to change our minds. This is only possible with a growth mindset. A fixed mindset will resist, avoid, or sidestep real change, sometimes even pretending that change has occurred.

Your identity is not set in stone — you're constantly engaging in constructive self-authorship, creating yourself anew every moment. Both your identity and your self-image are ongoing creative acts. In other words, who you are is not the result of your past, but something you choose — again and again.

The questions to ask yourself are: "Which mindset do I have?" and "Which mindset do I *want* to have?" All it takes to begin reshaping your psychology — and profoundly shifting your life experience — is your steadfast decision.

Shadow

There's a powerful realization, which comes from understanding that we create this world from the inside out. You contain it *all* — the light and the darkness, the bliss and the horror. This is not an easy truth to accept. If you feel a wave of resistance as you read the next sentence, know that it's perfectly normal. Your psyche contains all of the world's unspeakable atrocities; otherwise, you wouldn't be able to perceive them. Your shadow[50] is made up of those aspects of yourself and of human nature that you resist the most.

Behavioral aspects of your shadow include triggers, patterns, and projections. Triggers are the themes, subjects, or situations that evoke a strong negative emotional reaction and easily set you off. Patterns are the harmful habits, negative cycles, and "downward spirals" that make your state progressively worse. Projections are the ways you show up in the world — the masks you wear and the image you present to others.

You can relate to your shadow in one of three ways: resist it, succumb to it (hopefully not), or integrate it.

Most people resist their shadow. This doesn't solve anything; instead, it creates problems because the struggle takes place inside the person. Having caught early glimpses of their shadow — a frightening experience — many people try to "lock it away in the basement" like a wicked child, hoping no one will ever see their inner darkness. This suppression fuels inner resistance. Pushing against the darkness inside only takes you further away from the peace and coherence you seek.

Beyond the constant tension this creates, problems arise when the shadow inadvertently surfaces. The old fear leads to poor choices that recreate the unwanted scenario. Unaddressed aspects of the shadow keep showing up throughout one's life and become patterns, where the same painful experience emerges under new circumstances.

---

[50] Johnson, R.A. Owning Your Own Shadow: Understanding the Dark Side of the Psyche. HarperOne, 1991.

Succumbing to your shadow is rare. This happens when the fear of your inner darkness is so great that you become enslaved by it. This often involves "wearing masks" to convince others that your motives are noble. Traits like Machiavellianism, narcissism, or psychopathy can be seen as outcomes of giving in to one's shadow. In this case, the "wicked child" becomes the feared master, and the person ends up catering to the master's every whim while looking for ways to avoid being caught.

Integrating your shadow, on the other hand, is the most constructive path. It takes courage to acknowledge the darkness within you and face your fears. When you do this work, you discover that on the other side of what you fear most is a child — your younger self — who needs emotional support and a hug. The process of integration can be painful and emotional, but I assure you, it's worth it. Integrating your shadow is a way of healing, becoming whole. You realize that this child is not wicked at all — the neglected child simply needs love, as all children do. Integrating your shadow means embracing all aspects of yourself without giving in to their caprices. After all, you wouldn't let your four-year-old drive your car, no matter how big a tantrum he throws. One of the rewards for this work is that the energy once spent resisting your shadow becomes free for constructive and creative purposes. The benefits are profound.

What does integrating your shadow have to do with bliss? Like every other living organism, human beings operate in one of two modes: expansion or contraction[51]. Expansion begins with ease and

---

[51] Lipton, B.H., PhD. The Biology of Belief: Unleashing the Power of Consciousness, Matter, & Miracles. Hay House Inc., 2008.

leads to growth and creation. Contraction is driven by fear and results in closing off and protection. You can already guess which mode is a fertile ground for bliss — the other keeps genuine positive emotions out of reach. An unintegrated shadow, along with the constant inner resistance it creates, tends to keep you in the contraction mode, even if you don't realize it. The subtle fear that others might see what you're trying to hide continuously holds you in a protective state. To reach bliss, you must first find ease.

Tango offers a profound opportunity for introspection: each tanda can be seen as a symbolic encounter between archetypal energies — the Lover and the Warrior, the Caregiver and the Trickster. Each archetype carries a shadow aspect — a distorted, repressed, or exaggerated expression of its energy. Awareness of these polarities — and of their shadow sides — allows us to reconcile and balance them within ourselves, moving toward wholeness.

Carl Jung observed that when one pole dominates, the other becomes repressed into the unconscious, where it continues to influence us in hidden or destructive ways. For instance, a dancer who habitually overcontrols, insists, or dominates may be expressing an unbalanced inner Warrior, the archetype which embodies boundaries, structure, and clarity. This dancer's work, then, lies in evoking the Lover archetype — the capacity to yield, to trust, and to feel. Conversely, a dancer who easily surrenders and struggles to assert themselves may need to awaken the inner Warrior — to claim space (when teaching me how to walk, my tango teacher called it a *peaceful invasion*), to lead from grounded masculinity, and to move with clear intention.

The Lover embodies openness, sensuality, empathy, connection, and surrender — the capacity to feel deeply. When out of balance, the Lover seeks fusion rather than connection — clinging to the partner, absorbing the partner energetically, or confusing intimacy with sexuality. This often shows up as losing one's axis, seeking validation, or becoming overly attached to a particular partner or experience. For this archetype, integration lies in cultivating structure and self-containment: learning to stay open without losing one's center, to exchange energy while remaining grounded and present.

The Caregiver expresses nurturing, stability, and service, oriented toward the safety and well-being of others. When unbalanced, the Caregiver may constantly seek to please their partner, over-accommodate, apologize unnecessarily, or sacrifice their own needs for the comfort of their partner. This archetype has difficulty setting boundaries and saying *no*. Growth for this archetype involves allowing themselves to surrender and to receive — to be held, guided, and supported — thus restoring balance between giving and receiving. The Caregiver's breakthrough is the realization that self-care isn't selfish — it's essential.

The Caregiver's complement, the Trickster, brings humor, freedom, playfulness, and spontaneity. When out of balance, this energy can manifest as avoidance, distraction, manipulation, or fear of vulnerability — using humor to avoid authentic communication or emotional openness. This archetype's integration lies in transmuting play into awareness — using creativity to deepen connection instead of suppressing it, and using freedom to foster self-expression instead of escaping it.

> *"Until you make the unconscious conscious, it will direct your life and you will call it fate."*
> —C.G. Jung

When these archetypes are consciously recognized and brought into balance, tango becomes an alchemical process of integration — the sacred union of opposites. The goal isn't to eliminate the shadow, but to integrate it through conscious awareness. Shadow work in the context of the tango embrace becomes embodied individuation — a path toward recognizing, owning, reconciling, and balancing these aspects of one's psyche — a way of becoming whole.

If we zoom out and look at the social dynamics of the tango community, we'll find expressions of the shadow there as well. Every social group carries its own collective unconscious — and the tango community is no exception. Gossip, competition, exclusivity, and hierarchy all reflect the tango community's collective shadow. Simply becoming aware of these natural human patterns and social dynamics can support both individual and collective healing.

Trauma

The most important connection in your life is your connection with yourself. Without it, a genuine connection with others is impossible. But how can someone become disconnected from themselves? We are complex, multifaceted beings, and psychology has only begun to scratch the surface of the inner workings and intricacies of the human mind. Each of us is an incorporation of spiritual, emotional, psychological, and physical realms. In a perfect world, these realms integrate seamlessly, creating a healthy, whole individual. Our world, however, is still not perfect. Most of us are disconnected from ourselves in some regard — some simply to a lesser degree than others.

> *"Trauma disconnects us from ourselves. In trauma, our worldview becomes warped and our life becomes an attempt to somehow live through it to safety."*
> —Ayse Bombaci

Let's face it: most of us carry some form of trauma. Our life experiences have shaped us into who we are. On the one hand, this is reason for gratitude — loving yourself and being grateful for who you are is one of the most empowering outlooks you can have. On the other hand, unresolved trauma and an unhealed psyche can stand in the way of fully enjoying your life. An unhealed person often gets caught in cycles of re-traumatization, which keep ruining their health and relationships. Unhealed behavior leads to painful experiences that, in turn, surface again as unhealed behavior.

The coping mechanisms that once helped you survive eventually become a burden. The walls you built for protection turn into a prison. If your past dictates your present choices, you are not free. Healing — directing your energy, time, and attention toward becoming whole — is the path to freedom. At the heart of healing trauma is forgiveness. When you forgive, you let go, you become lighter. Healing asks that you sincerely forgive yourself and everyone who was involved, even those who hurt you. Your first thought may be that this is unfair, but remember: you're not doing it for them, you're doing it for *you*.

What does tango have to do with any of this? Tango awakens the psychosomatic intelligence of the body — the place where trauma and unprocessed feelings tend to reside. Trauma usually originates in our relationships or interactions with others; it can be seen as an embodied story. Tango, which emphasizes grounding and connection, allows you to rewrite these stories through movement in close connection with your partner.

> *"Lose your mind and come to your senses."*
> —Fritz Perls

In tango, even dancers who don't consciously identify with having psychosomatic issues often find that their bodies react unexpectedly when embraced a certain way or when dancing with particular partners. The body may tense, constrict, or withdraw in response to subtle cues — not because of the partner's actions, but because the body recognizes a feeling, a touch, or a posture that echoes past relational wounds. For instance, a dancer might notice their chest tightening when held too closely or experience a sudden fight-or-flight response when the connection feels overly dominant or submissive. This isn't necessarily a sign that the partner is doing something "wrong," but rather an opportunity to attune to the body's response and ask: "What story am I carrying in this space? What is this discomfort teaching me?"

Social tango, with its downright demand for authenticity and connection, can help you heal. Tango is a powerful catalyst — it magnifies and brings to the surface all of your un-dealt-with psycho-emotional baggage. The "dealing with it" part, however, is not so simple. I wholeheartedly encourage you to seek professional support to help resolve and heal trauma. You deserve to be happy.

The path of healing is not all moonlight and roses. Depending on the modality you choose, the process may at times be painful, but I assure you the outcome is worth it. The feelings of lightness, ease, and freedom you discover on your healing journey are exactly what you need to enjoy your life — and your tango — to the fullest.

What if You're Not Getting Invited?

This is one of the most common challenges in social tango. Everyone else seems to be dancing, yet no matter what you do, you're not getting the mirada or cabeceo. Other social dances approach invitations differently. At Latin dance parties, for instance, inviting someone "by hand" is common. In tango, however, hand invitations go against the códigos. At a milonga, mirada and cabeceo are comme il faut. While some see this as an outdated tradition, these customs ensure that both partners genuinely want to dance with each other. So what can you do if you're not getting invited?

The first step I recommend is to look closely at your worldview and beliefs — how you see yourself, others, and the outside world. I suggest starting here because your worldview and beliefs form the foundation of your entire experience, and social tango is no exception. Your worldview and your beliefs shape your habitual thoughts. Your thoughts shape your emotional state. Your emotional state, in turn, shapes your outward expression: your words, appearance, body language, movements, the way you walk, and the way you dance.

No matter how much you try to hide it, others pick up on your energy — on what you transmit out into the world. Some people are more sensitive to it than others, but the unintentional message usually comes through, regardless of how well you think you conceal it.

On and around the dance floor, we become even more exposed. Social tango magnifies and reveals our character — our strengths and our flaws alike.

Here are some examples of limiting beliefs and their constructive counterparts:

"What I want matters more than what other people want." This belief lacks empathy and care for others. At your core, you are no different from anyone else. A constructive belief would be: "I care about what others want just as much as I care about what I want." This creates more win-win situations, where both partners share equal desire — an important condition for euphoria.

"It's acceptable to manipulate or take advantage of others to get what I want." This belief lacks respect. The Golden Rule applies here: do unto others as you would want them to do unto you. A constructive belief would be: "Being open, honest, and authentic with others is the best way to get what I want."

"In order to get what I want, I have to compete with other people." This belief confuses social tango with sports. A constructive belief would be: "At a milonga, we are all on the same team."

These are just a few examples to give you an idea of how your worldview shapes your experience at a milonga. The way you regard others will directly influence how interested they are in dancing with you.

If your automatic reaction to not being invited is self-judgment, try to reframe such moments as opportunities for self-inquiry. Social tango has a way of revealing limiting belief patterns and emotional wounds, allowing you to notice that which no longer serves you.

You might ask yourself gentle, reflective questions such as, "Am I projecting an old narrative onto a new situation?" or "What part of me feels unseen right now?" Approaching these experiences with genuine curiosity and kindness can help you heal your relationship with essential qualities like openness, self-acceptance, and self-love.

The next step I recommend is taking group classes. The first and most obvious benefit is that learning improves your tango, making you a better and more sought-after partner. Second, group classes build your adaptability. In most cases, the format involves changing partners every few compositions, which hones your ability to adjust to different partners — an essential skill in social tango. And third, group classes give you the chance to meet and connect with others who are "in the same boat." It's a wonderful way to make friends, find your practice partners, and expand your social presence in the local tango scene.

A *No* as a Gift

How often has this happened: we accept a proposal, agree to a venture, or take on a project not because we truly want to, but out of some vague sense of duty — or perhaps just courtesy — and later regret not having said *no*? From an early age, many of us are conditioned to see anything we do for ourselves, rather than for others, as selfish. As a result, we often place the well-being of others above our own. The unspoken rules of social interaction, shaped by conditional love, suggest that refusing an unwanted proposal makes us self-centered and somehow indebted to the world. Saying yes and acting altruistically, on the other hand, makes it seem as though the world now owes us something. Absurd as it may sound, this unconscious dynamic is the cause of many of our troubles.

Social tango shines a light on this pattern and offers a chance to rethink this approach entirely. Even those who dislike — or feel unable — to say *no* will quickly find they must do so at milongas, or they won't last very long. But saying *no* is not easy. For many people, it's a sensitive issue, influenced by at least three key factors.

First, when saying *no*, many of us fear that others will notice this and stop inviting us. In my opinion, this underestimates others. A more empowering perspective is: "When others see that I say *no* — that I am being selective — they will be even more interested in inviting me."

I once experienced this at my favorite milonga. A "new girl" stood by the dance floor, quietly looking around. I hesitated to invite her, as I hadn't yet seen her dance. My indecision vanished in an instant when I observed what happened next. Only a few people were around the dance floor when a tanda began. A young man approached her from the side, stopped about two meters away, and leaned forward in an exaggerated attempt to catch her gaze. The girl noticed this "cabeceo" from the corner of her eye and promptly turned away to show she wasn't interested. I concluded that, since she had the confidence to refuse such a clumsy invitation, she must be selective — and therefore likely a good dancer. Taking my time, I walked around the dance floor, invited her properly from across the room, and then praised my intuition for two tandas in a row.

Second, we often associate a *no* with non-love, punishment, or even disavowal. After all, refusal can be a powerful tool in the hands of a manipulator. Yet the truth is that how we perceive a refusal is a matter of perspective. A *no* has nothing to do with these sentiments — it can be seen in a very different light.

Third, we do not like receiving a *no* from others. But this, too, is a matter of perspective. A *no* can be seen as a gift, because the alternative — someone accepting against their genuine desire — is far less desirable. In this sense, refusal is actually a win-win: both people end up in a better situation than if the refuser had accepted.

A *no* is much better than an "okay, fine." The latter is nothing other than condescension. When someone hears a *no*, they can feel the tone and emotion of the refusal, so naturally different kinds of refusals are received differently. But even a meek but honest *no* is far better than a feigned or reluctant "okay" (unless, of course, it's part of a playful exchange between old friends).

A clear *no* during cabeceo is also better than pretending not to notice. A wonderful tanguera taught me this way of communicating at my first festival. If you see someone looking at you but don't want to dance with them, meet their eyes and then look down. This is a cabeceo *no*. Why is this better than pretending to not notice? The answer is simple: a timely *no* gives both of you the chance to invite someone else for this tanda.

At a festival, I once spoke with a tanguero who complained that many women were refusing him: "They don't even understand what they're doing — if I look at a woman and she tells me *no*, then I'm not going to invite anyone else for that tanda!" He explained his reasoning as respect for his chosen partner, emphasizing the importance and precision of his choice. But to me, this sounded like manipulation. By declaring, "It's you or no one else," he was loading his proposal with a condition and placing responsibility for his well-being on the other person: "Now it's your fault that I'm sitting out this tanda!"

Of course, simply having the chance to invite someone else doesn't guarantee success. At one marathon, I received the funniest *no* of my life. I tried to cabeceo a tanguera I had never met, but she didn't notice me. Fine, that happens. Soon I shifted my gaze to a friend sitting a little closer. She caught my look and said, "I thought you were trying to cabeceo someone else? Keep cabeceo-ing her!"

A *no* does not mean that something has to change between two people, nor that some kind of "sanctions" must be imposed to restore justice. Imagine you're serving homemade cocktails at a party. You want your guests to enjoy themselves. Would you be offended if someone said, "No, thank you"? Would you then stubbornly refuse to try the homemade cake they brought? Of course not.

Oftentimes, to soften a refusal, I feel tempted to explain myself — but it's better not to. "No, thank you." Full stop. It's not easy, but it's the best option for both of us. Explanations usually serve only to ease guilt, and I don't believe we should feel guilty for saying *no*. After all, is lack of desire a crime? There may be countless reasons for refusing, but in the end none of them matter — they all come down to a lack of desire in the moment.

If I'm afraid to tell her *no*, it means that on some level I'm underestimating her, imagining she is too fragile to handle it. It means I fear she might misunderstand me or take offense, and by doing so I'm subconsciously ascribing negative qualities to her. In reality, she is perfectly capable of taking my *no* constructively. Her reaction is her choice. And if she chooses to take offense, that only confirms my intuition was right.

If you think about it, we actually refuse far more often than we accept. When a tanda begins, and I lead someone onto the dance floor, it effectively means I've just refused everyone else at the milonga!

Tango is a miniature model of life, a social game that invites us to look inward. If we notice something we don't like, we have the chance to change and grow. Every person in our life is a mirror. In social tango, this analogy is especially true, because interaction with our partner happens quickly and on many levels at once. Learning to say *no* and to accept refusal are essential skills — and social tango offers endless opportunities to practice them, while learning to accept only the invitations we genuinely desire.

Dealing with a Tango Low

A friend once asked me, "What do you do when suddenly it feels like whatever you do on the dance floor — nothing seems to work?"

A "tango low" can be deeply discouraging. I know — I've been there. I vividly recall a moment at a milonga when it felt as if I couldn't even take basic steps in a tango embrace. I looked down, almost bewildered, to find that I had legs, with feet attached to them.

A tango low is a time when it seems you've forgotten everything you know — steps, figures, axis, embrace, all of it. On a graph of progress, it looks like a dip, an apparent regression in your learning curve. But what is it, really?

Walking sounds like a simple activity, doesn't it? Yet it's one of the most complex tasks in terms of biomechanics. You learned to walk around the age of one, and ever since you've been walking on autopilot. Then, years later, along comes a tango teacher who shows you how to walk all over again — this time drawing your attention to every tiny detail of each stage of a step: "Here you push; here you hold — don't collapse; here you dissociate." But you've been walking your whole life! When it comes to the body, learning something new requires unlearning decades of old habits. And that's not so straightforward.

This is true for most, if not all, aspects of body mechanics. We don't truly learn new movements; we refine and change the way we've been moving all along. The human body is a finite instrument, and unlearning the "old way" is an inevitable part of learning anything new. This process takes time, and progress is never linear. Unlearning often shows up as one or more "tango lows" — times when, usually at a milonga and often when you least expect it, your body suddenly makes it clear that you've unlearned the "old thing." Great. But shouldn't you be doing the "new thing" now?

I wish it were that easy. Learning takes time, and during a tango low it may feel as if you can't do either — the old *or* the new thing. This can feel quite discouraging.

So what should you do the next time you experience a tango low? Celebrate! It means your learning is starting to take root. Here are a few practical things you can do to support your body in the process:

1. Record a summary of every lesson — write it down, or make a voice or video note, whatever works best for you. When you hit a tango low, you can review your last lessons and pinpoint the

topic your body is currently "processing." Practice the new thing as soon as you have an opportunity.
2. Go to a práctica. Ask a friend to join you, or find a partner who also wants to practice.
3. Take another lesson. Even if it's a group class on a different topic, your tango low may actually be the perfect chance to absorb something new — because your body has just let go of something that wasn't working.
4. Go to a milonga and try to have fun, no matter how clumsy you feel. The duration of your tango low will largely depend on your attitude toward it.

Whatever you do, give yourself time. Remember, you're asking your body to change something it's been doing for years. You're literally rewiring your brain and creating new neural pathways. Be kind to yourself and trust your body's ability to learn. It will reward you with plenty of dopamine and oxytocin.

Your Temple

If you reflect on the fleeting nature of our existence in this world, you'll realize that nothing here really belongs to you except your physical body. It is the only thing you truly own for the duration of your life. How you treat your body — how you care for it, condition it, what you put into it, and even how you speak to it — is the way your body will treat you.

Your body is your temple, and your health and well-being should always be your highest priority. If this is not the case, and you neglect or indefinitely postpone caring for your body, it may eventually resort to asserting its due place at the top of your priority list. Our bodies usually do this by getting sick. Without health and well-being, all other priorities lose their meaning and become unfulfilling. It's far more effective to prioritize caring for your body while you're healthy: get enough sleep, drink plenty of water, eat nourishing food, spend time outdoors, and exercise.

Of course, there are no guarantees in life. Accidents in social tango happen, and sometimes they cause physical pain. No matter how carefully we follow navigation rules, we cannot fully avoid this. What we can avoid is aggravating the injury with subsequent psychological self-poisoning. I'm referring to those moments when our default reaction, left uncontrolled, grows from irritation into anger or even a grudge. We hold onto the dissonance, keeping it inside with some subconscious aim — perhaps to prove the world isn't perfect, or in some hope of restoring justice. But clinging to anger or grudges rarely achieves these aims, and it almost always damages our mood and health.

So what are the alternatives? I believe the most constructive response to an accident on the dance floor is to apologize sincerely and to mentally forgive everyone involved, including yourself. This applies regardless of whose fault it was or who is in pain. Sincerity is key. First, by apologizing we acknowledge that something *unwanted* has happened. Second, we affirm that it wasn't intentional. Third, by expressing regret, we release the dissonance instead of holding onto it. And fourth, by setting an example, we invite others involved to do the same.

So why don't we always apologize? Sometimes the hit is minor — no big deal. Sometimes we don't want to interrupt the dance. In these cases, the incident is left unresolved, "as is." More often than not, it feels easier to assume the other couple is at fault. "Why should I apologize? It's me — or my partner — who's in pain. They're the ones who should apologize." Unfortunately, many of us see apologizing as something embarrassing, especially when it isn't clear who is to blame.

I try to approach this differently. When I apologize, I express my regret that the incident happened at all. I take full responsibility for *having been part of it*, without trying to assign blame or restore justice. Even if it wasn't my fault, I'm just as sorry for having been involved as I would be if I had caused the mishap. I don't wait for their apology. Their response is entirely their choice. And if I'm the one in pain, then by apologizing I also ask forgiveness of my own body. In Hawaiian healing practice Ho'oponopono[52], for example, the process comes down to repeating the phrases:

"Thank you. I'm sorry. Please forgive me. I love you."

By saying "thank you," I express gratitude to my body for communicating with me, even if in such an unfortunate way. "I'm sorry" that this incident occurred. "Please forgive me" for having been part of it. "I love you" affirms my love for every cell of my body.

There are countless parallels between life and tango, and this one is vital: safety first. Safety is more important than musicality, more important than comfort. In social tango we are never alone, and while we cannot control the choices of others, we always have the

---

[52] Vitale, J. & Len, I.H. Zero Limits: The Secret Hawaiian System for Wealth, Health, Peace, and More. Wiley (John Wiley & Sons, Inc.), 2007.

right to choose our own actions — regarding safety, responsibility, and even our state.

Your care for your body begins with your attitude toward it. Your habitual thoughts and underlying beliefs create the vibrational environment that shapes both your physical state and the situations you typically encounter. We are always programming our subconscious, whether we realize it or not. The question is: are you programming yourself for desired or undesired scenarios? If you subconsciously think of your body as a burden, it will give you more reasons to feel frustrated. But if you think of your body as your most treasured possession, it will reward you generously. Conditioned with a positive vibrational environment, your body will be ready to take you to the ninth cloud the moment you hear tango music.

Humor

Humor, in most of its forms, is one of the best tools for handling difficult social situations. Beyond releasing happiness hormones and being good for your health, laughter eases tension and makes it easier to let go of what might otherwise upset you. Whenever humor is a possible response, I tend to choose it — even before considering the other options.

Of course, there's a fine line between laughing *with* someone and laughing *at* them. The former is humor at its best; the latter is a form of aggression and should be avoided altogether. If you're unsure whether your joke might hurt someone, don't say it. It's not worth the chuckle.

Your true power lies in how you respond to situations. One evening I danced several tandas with one of my favorite partners. I also invited her for the last tanda, and she agreed — just as we both noticed another leader who had hoped to dance with her. He hadn't had a chance yet, and he saw clearly that it wasn't my first time dancing with her that night. As I led her to the floor, he joked, "Oh good — at least you got to dance with her!" All three of us laughed. Could he have gotten upset? Of course. But instead he chose humor, dissolving any negativity and setting a wonderful example of how to respond in moments like this. Remember, it's only tango.

"Laughter is proof of intelligence. It's the mind recognizing absurdity and choosing joy over confusion, a small rebellion that makes us both wiser and kinder."
—Stephen Fry

The highest form of humor is your ability to laugh at yourself. Your world is a reflection of your inner universe, so when you choose the subject of your joke, why not go straight to the source? Don't take yourself too seriously. An easygoing spirit shows real strength of character. At a milonga, allow yourself to laugh and enjoy as much as possible. When you're having fun, you're quite close to experiencing bliss.

Connection, Communication, and Intimacy

One of my favorite pathways to bliss in social tango is non-verbal communication. Outside of dance, this is rarely practiced, and many people don't even realize it's possible. In tango, we dance by communicating, and we communicate by dancing. Tango allows you to learn a great deal about another person without either of you saying a word. Verbal communication allows you to create intricate mazes of words and meaning, where your partner can easily get lost. Non-verbal communication is more direct and honest. As Shakira puts it, "hips don't lie."

True intimacy can only exist in an atmosphere of authentic communication. Social tango creates a unique space where two people can be as open and real with each other as they choose. Most of us yearn for intimacy, yet — outside of exceptional relationships and friendships — true intimacy is often lacking in our lives. This experience of intimacy is a major reason why people stay in tango, despite its steep learning curve, and why they keep returning to lessons, prácticas, and milongas. Tango offers the chance to experience intimacy every time we dance, and to explore it as deeply as we wish.

Intimacy, of course, should not be confused with sexuality. Sexuality is when the focus is on physical pleasure, while intimacy is about emotions, mind, and soul. Sexuality is a beautiful thing, and tango can be as sexual as both partners may want it to be. However, when it is one-sided — coming from only one partner — sexuality can feel invasive, violating, and unwelcome to the other. For a woman to relax into her feminine energy and enjoy the dance, she needs to feel safe. Above all, this means feeling safe with her partner, and unwanted sexuality is the polar opposite of the safety a man is responsible for creating.

Contrary to what some may assume, consent in social tango is not limited to agreeing to dance with each other. It also includes the choice between a close or open embrace. If one partner prefers close embrace while the other prefers open, the open embrace takes precedence, as it is safer and less intimate. This is especially important when dancing with someone for the first time. When a tanda begins, your responsibility is to pay close attention to the embrace your partner chooses. This is a key part of tuning in — sensing what they want. If your partner feels comfortable with you, they may invite you to close the embrace at some point, but they are never obligated to do so. And even if they do, they don't have to keep it closed. If either partner senses that something is off in the dance, their natural instinct is to open the embrace. This is why it's essential to recognize when your partner wants to open the embrace, and to always respect that choice.

Real intimacy can only happen when both partners consciously create an inner environment that welcomes authentic communication. Because of its more innocent nature compared to sexuality, intimacy in its truest sense is a much more common goal in tango. Social tango provides the framework — it sets the stage, establishes the boundaries and rules, and offers the means to communicate. *What you communicate is entirely up to you.*

Intimacy begins with desire, and connection is the path to fulfill it. It is the longing to both get to know another person and to open up, to allow yourself to be seen. Your character with all its flaws and imperfections, your fears, quirks, and pet peeves — all of this seeks recognition in another. We all want to be accepted and loved, which is why authentic intimacy is so precious. Intimacy is the experience of being accepted and welcomed into another person's inner world. It allows us to truly see one another and to share in a joyful exchange. At its deepest, intimacy allows us to view life from another's perspective, to be so attuned to our partner that we experience a sense of oneness.

A genuine connection with another person is invaluable. The purpose of real dialogue is twofold: to understand and to be understood. Beneath that, however, lies the deeper desire to connect. The most precious moments arise when you connect on a level you haven't experienced before. A genuine connection is created when you recognize yourself in your partner — when you realize you're looking into a metaphorical mirror. By being authentic and open, you create the space for true dialogue, and it is through dialogue that genuine connection can be established.

Argentinian folklore dances like Chacarera and Zamba offer a slightly different path for two people to interact. In these dances, connection is established almost entirely through eye contact, with little or no physical touch whatsoever. At first glance, this may seem more superficial than the physical connection in tango. Nothing could be further from the truth. From first-hand experience, I can assure you that the depth of connection created through eye contact in Argentinian folklore can be as profound as you are willing to explore.

EYE-GAZING EXERCISE

Set aside 20–30 minutes for this exercise. Sit comfortably facing your partner, about 60 to 80 centimeters apart. Both of you should do the same thing: look into each other's eyes with the intention of connecting, of seeing deeply into your partner. At the same time, allow yourself to soften and open up — allow yourself to be seen. Stay relaxed. It's fine to switch from one eye to the other, and it's fine to blink — this isn't a staring contest. Whatever emotions arise, let them come. Acknowledge them mentally and feel them fully while maintaining the connection. The purpose of this exercise is to explore how deeply you can connect with another person and how much you can allow yourself to open.

Connection through eye contact is another important reason to use mirada and cabeceo. Eye contact with your partner, no matter how brief, is the best way to begin your dance. A mirada is far less intrusive than other ways of inviting, because it doesn't demand a response. What better way to start your tanda than with the softest way to communicate your interest? Because of its gentle nature, cabeceo also conveys genuine care and respect for the other person, which is appealing in itself. Simply expressing your desire to dance with someone through eye contact — and receiving their reciprocation — can feel wonderful and has the potential to set the tone for the entire tanda. This is how blissful dances often begin.

The Medium and the Protocol

The tango embrace is the medium of our communication. Is the embrace light as a feather, or does it envelop you like a weighted blanket? The flexibility of our upper bodies, the tone, and the level of our muscular engagement all shape the quality of the embrace. Beneath these qualities lies your intention — what do you want to communicate to your partner with your embrace?

The key components of communication are signaling and perceiving. Through your muscle tone — the degree of engagement of your muscle groups — you make your body available for your partner's perception. By consciously articulating, expanding, and contracting the spirals in your body, keeping your figure aligned, and maintaining a specific amount of tone, you give your partner all the information they need to perceive your body in space. This helps create a dynamic 3D model of your body in your partner's mind, allowing them to sense where your body and limbs are at any moment without having to look down.

Your partner can *feel into* your body on one key condition: they can only feel what you communicate. If a part of your body lacks the right amount of tone, your partner cannot perceive it. For example, if you drop the connection in your shoulder blade, that part of your body essentially disappears from your partner's radar. Signaling, then, means using a moderate level of tone to convey your body's shape, position, and direction — making yourself "visible" to your partner.

So what's the right amount of tone? There's no need to tense up — in fact, that would be counterproductive. The baseline for your signal is surprisingly low. It can simply be a non-verbal declaration of your "I am" presence. When you embrace your partner, simply tell them with your body, "I'm here." When you take a step, let it say, "I'm going there." It's about taking up space and owning it, allowing your *intention* to create the right amount of tone in your body. Think of muscle tone as the *protocol* of your communication, through which both partners' intentions are communicated.

Whether at prácticas or milongas, pay close attention to your embrace. With practice, you'll learn to vary and play with the amount of tone you offer your partner, "coloring" your signal to reflect the music, your mood, or anything else you wish to express. Conversely, if your goal is to better perceive your partner's signals, practice will heighten your sensitivity to shifts in your partner's tone. This will enable you to pick up on the more subtle and nuanced signals they offer.

Abstractions

Of course, we don't consciously adjust the tone levels in individual muscle groups in order to communicate. If the embrace is the medium and muscle tone is the protocol, then what are the higher-level means of our communication? Much like the "I am here" declaration, we can embody visualizations and abstract ideas with the intent to communicate. With a bit of practice, these ideas will naturally transmit through your tone and embrace. Here are some abstractions that may help you communicate non-verbally.

- "My partner and I stand still, while pushing the world together in the direction opposite of where we're going." This visualization helps improve synchronicity, allowing you and your partner to move together.
- "I got it!" and "You have it!" Similar to team sports like volleyball, you can communicate your intention to take on the next movement ("I got it!") or, conversely, to give space for your partner to do so ("You have it!"). This involves saying the phrase silently to yourself and letting your body express it. Besides being fun, this approach helps prevent you and your partner from clashing.
- "Wait for me." Similar to "I got it," this conveys a request: "Give me a moment, set the music aside for a bit." It can be especially helpful with a "runaway" partner or someone who tends to prioritize the music above all else.
- "Are you ready? Let's go!" This is useful when shifting from a softer to a more toned embrace, often to accelerate and interpret a dynamic variación. One of my teachers offered a helpful visual: imagine that your embrace is a beach ball you're softly holding in the water, at the level where the ball comfortably floats on the surface. Communicating "we're about to speed up," is like submerging the ball halfway into the water. To do this, you need to slightly lower your vertical level, and gently increase your muscle tone — otherwise you will lose the ball. Lowering your level by just a couple of centimeters also lowers the couple's center of gravity, allowing quicker, more effective steps. American football players, for example, know that to be able to change direction quickly, they have to get low and closer to the ground.
- Communication via the main spirals of your body. This form of communication flourishes in close embrace, when your torsos

are directly connected in front. It matters because the main spirals in your body are congruent with those of your partner. In close embrace, the two of you are essentially dissociating around a shared axis — the axis of the couple. You communicate by engaging and releasing your individual spirals, alternating between association and dissociation. The leader's engaged spiral invites a mirrored response from the follower, evoking a congruent spiral to form in return. Two keys are essential here. First, remember that energy comes from the floor. To communicate this way, both partners must push the floor and transfer the energy from the floor into the shared spiral. Second, *both* partners must engage and release their individual spirals — each partner's dissociation plays a vital role.

- Communication via the preparatory stage of movement. In Pilates, for example, a teacher might ask you to first *think* about raising your leg before actually raising it. As you focus on the movement you're about to make, your muscles begin to prepare. In the same way, when a leader thinks of initiating a movement, subtle shifts occur in their body — recall the counterforce vector we discussed in *Controlled Movement*. The follower subconsciously picks up on these subtle changes, and their body begins to prepare in response. While this requires sensitivity, it's a skill that can be developed with practice and determination. This type of communication allows partners to attune to each other on a very fine level — this is the magic of true synchronization, where it feels as if the dancers are reading each other's minds.

- Communication via our focus of attention. It's easy to imagine focusing your attention on an object — you do it every time you look at something. A more abstract idea is that you can also direct your attention to any point in space: inside your body, in front, behind, or anywhere around you. This doesn't require looking at the chosen point, though your natural tendency may be to turn your head a little or slightly lean toward it. You can also *move* the focus of your attention within the three-dimensional space around you. Communication via your focus of attention means allowing this dynamic visualization to change the tone of your body, which serves as a signal to your partner. Your partner can perceive these signals and sense with surprising accuracy where your attention is focused, the direction it is moving, and how quickly. Again, sensitivity increases with intention and practice. This form of communication is part of the magic behind the precision of movements achieved by revered tango maestros.

Obstacles

What can interfere with non-verbal communication in tango? Here are some possible obstacles to consider.

- Your goals differ too much from those of your partner. For example, one partner is extrinsically, the other — intrinsically motivated. Or perhaps you want to connect deeply with your partner, while they are scanning the room for their next partner. Many such scenarios can arise, and all of them get in the way of communication.
- Your degree of openness is not aligned with that of your partner. If one partner is closed off and their degree of openness is below a certain threshold, communication will not take place. The reasons may vary from past trauma, to fear of intimacy, to simply being distant or distracted in the moment.

- Your levels of sensitivity are mismatched. If one partner's sensitivity is too low, no matter how much effort the other puts in, a true dialogue will not happen. Inexperience may play a role here, though it isn't always the case.
- A partner's psycho-emotional state can easily become an obstacle to communication. For example, if they can't switch off their "work mode," are preoccupied with their relationship issues, or are under emotional distress.
- Physical strain, pain, exhaustion, or sleepiness can also get in the way. The body may still be moving, but the dance will lack substance.
- "Noise" takes many forms: stiffness, tension, lack of muscle tone, unnecessary movements, or automatic motions. All of these can drown out the signal. The main cause of noise is simply not realizing you're creating it. Whether the "noisy" partner is on autopilot or has bad habits — like pushing or pulling with the arm or "hanging" on their partner — communication will be difficult, if not impossible. The remedy is straightforward: discovery, intention, lessons, technique, and practice. First identify the issues, then focus on correcting them.
- Instability, as described in *Stability and Technique*, turns your dance into partner management and prevents meaningful communication altogether. The solution, as with noise, is technique, lessons, and practicas.

"Yes!" – an Antidote to Mistakes

One of the pathways to euphoria is the call-and-response of constant confirmation between partners. Suggesting a movement and having your partner respond exactly as you imagined brings immense satisfaction. This steady flow of *yes* creates a shared experience of joy. Since movement is a function of time, this confirmation becomes a continuous, elevated experience for both partners. For example, if after a long discussion we finally agree on something, the *yes* feels like a single peak. In social tango, however, the confirmation — and bliss — can be continuous: "Yes, you understood me," "Yes, I understood you," repeated moment after moment. And it's not a *yes* to the same thing — it's a *yes* to something new every moment, because every instant in our dance is unique.

This ongoing bidirectional confirmation generates feelings of acceptance and safety in both partners. Unfortunately, it's not as common as one would hope. Less experienced dancers often fear making mistakes on the dance floor. Modern culture tends to glorify perfection and stigmatize mistakes, so this fear can run deep. A more helpful perspective is to remember that in social tango there are no mistakes. This isn't a test — you're out having fun, no one cares! Tango is not a science, it's an art. The difference between a "mistake" and an "alternative choice" is simply your *attitude* toward it. In social tango something can be perceived as a mistake only if it creates the feelings of criticism, blame, or guilt. Again, perception is a choice. Without those reactions, when your attitude projects total acceptance, your dance becomes carefree and primes both partners for a delightful experience.

> *"Nothing will stop you from being creative more effectively as the fear of making a mistake."*
> —John Cleese

Allow both yourself and your partner to be imperfect. Finding beauty in imperfections, giving yourselves permission to play and have fun, brings you closer to your goal. Let go of heavy burdens of expectations, judgments, and perfectionism. Release, let go, set yourself free!

The feeling of genuine connection and intimacy with another creates a joyful space where everything becomes possible. Your personal limitations fall away, and you stop seeing yourself through the lens of your ego. This allows you to enter the "now," to come back to the present moment[53], which contains nothing but bliss. Perhaps counterintuitively, surrendering control makes you more creative. Without the need to dictate how things have to unfold, and with your ego no longer in charge, the possibilities become infinite. Genuine connection and intimacy open the door to the "flow" state, making bliss readily available to both you and your partner.

Partner

Tango is, above all, a partnership — a collaboration. The possibilities of this partnership expand when you genuinely appreciate your partner, rather than viewing them simply as a ticket to enter the ronda. Your partner isn't there just so you can keep count or look good. The person in your arms is a gift to be appreciated, an opportunity to co-create something wonderful. The fact that they chose you — to be close, to share their skill, attention, and emotions with

---

[53] Tolle, E. The Power of Now: A Guide to Spiritual Enlightenment (Novato, CA: New World Library, 1999).

you — deserves your awareness, gratitude, and respect. It's often said that a tanda is a marriage that lasts twelve minutes. In those minutes, you enter a miniature relationship, and the way you perceive your partner shapes the experience for both of you.

In tango, your choice of partner matters more than in many other social dances. Technically, this is because partners often share their axes, which is not a simple task. If one partner struggles with stability or technique, the other can compensate to some extent. But when it comes to goals — why are we dancing right now, and what do we want to achieve? — that compensation creates an imbalance in favor of the less skilled partner. There's nothing wrong with dancing with beginners; in fact, I encourage it as a way to contribute to your local tango community. Dancing with partners of all levels is valuable, as it offers opportunities for both partners to learn. Still, relying on your partner's skills, balance, and technique in the long term is a losing strategy, because it turns you into a "taker." Dancing with a skilled partner may feel good, but in order to reach euphoria, you have to possess those skills as well. In other words, there are no good ways to bypass classes, technique workshops, and practicas. True enjoyment of tango is not only about finding a good partner — it's about becoming a good partner yourself.

Another helpful question to ask yourself while dancing is, "Is this for me, or for my partner?" Tango mirrors life in many ways, and this one is essential. The joy you feel when you realize you're making your partner happy by sensing what they want and giving it to them is unlike anything else. If your goal is to make your partner feel good, you're definitely on the right track. And if your partner shares the same intention? That's when the magic happens. This is the true reason tango is a partner dance. It's not only that some figures can't be done alone — it's that 1 + 1 can become more than 2. Tango is about partnership, synergy, and the magic that arises when each person is focused on the other's joy. Contrast that with *using your partner* to feel good yourself — sounds sketchy, doesn't it? A tanguera friend once described such an account with a rhetorical question: "Why should I dance with you if our dance is going to be all about *you* again?"

Yet another way to think about the collaborative side of tango is not by asking, "Which partner is this for?" but rather, "What am I bringing to the table?" If I am open, honest, and caring, and if I give one hundred percent of myself to the dance without reservation, then my partner will surely enjoy it. My goals don't need to be centered on my partner's pleasure; I simply take care of my part of the equation. If I give it my all, this will invite my partner to do the same, and we are sure to have a good time.

Think of it like giving a gift to someone you love. Watching their face light up, seeing their smile and excitement fills you with joy. That same feeling arises when you come to a milonga with the intention to share, to give yourself fully, without holding anything back. The attitude of giving and sharing is both the essence of tango and a key to a fulfilling life.

It's much easier to reach your goal for this tanda when your partner's goal aligns with yours — or at least when both goals point in a similar direction. You are unlikely to experience "cloud nine" bliss with a partner who, for example, is busy looking in the mirror, preoccupied with the aesthetics of their dance.

To a beginner, flashy moves at a milonga may seem dazzling. With years of experience, however, comes a different understanding — "Not all that glitters is gold." In many cases, dancing with a showy partner isn't particularly enjoyable. Bliss is rarely flashy; to an onlooker, the bliss shared inside a couple can even appear dull. Subtle movements, simple steps, slow-downs, and pauses may look like little from the outside. To recognize "gold," you have to look deeper, pay attention to the qualities of their movements, and see if you can "ride their wave" just by observing their dance. Seek, and you shall find.

Choice

"Do you dance with everyone, or only with your friends?" It's not the first time I've heard this question. The real issue isn't the black-and-white fallacy of the question itself, but the deeper subject to which it points.

Choice plays an essential role in tango: choosing which milonga to attend, choosing where to spend time at a milonga and whom to talk to, choosing whom to invite for a tanda, choosing how to move in a given moment. In truth, we are making choices every moment of our lives. Existentialism suggests that everything is a choice — it's just that most of the time we make these choices without our direct awareness.

My aim is to make conscious choices guided by my feelings every instant. This allows me to be in the moment, to be fully here and now. Choice, based on personal feelings, is the foundation of authenticity — and that's exactly what I'm looking for.

Do I dance with everyone, or only with my friends? I can tell you how I choose whom to invite — I pay close attention to my feelings.

It's really not complicated. When the music begins, I choose what feels best. We all have the ability to imagine the feelings we're likely to experience from events that haven't yet occurred. A simple example: everyone knows what it's like to choose a meal at a restaurant. Given the options, we pick what we believe will bring us the most enjoyment.

And yes, sometimes the partner I hoped to invite is already dancing this beautiful tanda with someone else. C'est la vie. At that point, I face another choice: I can get upset, stew in my emotions, and leave, or I can wait for the proper Pugliese tanda, invite a wonderful partner to dance, and leave all this drama and unfairness on the dance floor.

Everything we do, every action we take, we ultimately do in order to feel better. Even when we know this choice may bring negative emotions, we make this choice to live up to certain principles or norms, or to conform to someone's expectations. The promise of this conformity and belonging, in return, makes us feel better. When a tanda begins and I'm deciding whom to invite, my goal is simply to make the choice that feels best in its own right, without detours through conformity.

The only real obstacle to following our emotional navigation system is fear. When we give in to fear and focus on what we want to avoid, we paint ourselves into a corner.

> *"Any action prompted by fear leads to the exact outcome you're afraid of."*
> —Dr. Sky Blossoms

Bound by the constraints of other people's expectations, we lose the ability to take any action at all. One very good leader left tango entirely because he believed he was obliged to dance with everyone — and this was physically impossible. "It's unbearable! They're all looking at me, like…"

But won't people judge me if I refuse them? They might. And if you truly respect them, you'll allow them to feel the way they choose. What is always up to you, however, is *how* you say *no*. We'll explore this further in the section on *Kindness*.

Since much of your joy in tango comes from bringing enjoyment to your partner, here's something that can help when choosing whom to invite — be curious. What is her emotional state right now? Is she enjoying a conversation with a friend? Are her feet sore, and does she need a rest? For some, sensing another person's state of mind can feel challenging, but your curiosity — your genuine desire to know — can help you develop this skill and produce positive results. Keep in mind that people's moods can change, even during a milonga. If you're like me and tend to have a bit of a know-it-all attitude, it's especially important to learn how to set it aside and remain curious.

In social tango there are also many people on the other side of the sensitivity spectrum — those who feel the emotions of others a bit too strongly. The mood of people around them tends to affect them directly, whether they want it or not. At a crowded milonga this can quickly become overwhelming. A partner's mood can easily rub off on an empath, especially after sharing an embrace for twelve minutes. For this highly sensitive group, the challenge is learning to distinguish their own emotions from those of others.

For most of us, curiosity is the most helpful attitude when choosing a partner. At the same time, it's important to make your own emotional state available to others — to "open up," so to speak. This doesn't mean you need to put your emotions on display, but if you tend to close off in social situations, it's worth doing a quick self-check at a milonga. What is your body language saying to your potential partners? Social tango offers plenty of opportunities to develop emotional intelligence, no matter where you fall on the sensitivity spectrum. We are always communicating non-verbally, and our emotional state plays a central role in this communication.

The dance floor is a safe space to express emotions, a way for both of you to enrich the moment with new "colors." You want to let your potential partner decide whether they wish to be part of it or not. An invitation is an opportunity, a potential to be realized only when there is genuine desire on both sides.

Invitation

Even when I consider my potential partner's state, I still rely on my own feelings when deciding whether to invite her or not.

The look in someone's eyes always reveals their emotions. If they try to hide their emotions, you can sense that they are closed off. If they wear a mask, the pretense is obvious. If an actress fails to fully feel a given emotion, she won't be able to make the audience feel it either. The "why haven't we danced yet?" look of reproach is very different from the "let's dance this one!" sparkle in the eyes. Entire books and studies exist on body language, but deep analysis isn't really necessary — it's enough to simply want to sense what the person is feeling in the moment.

The quality of the invitation sets the emotional tone for the entire tanda. Invitations can be formal or informal, lighthearted (my personal favorite), or bittersweet, when the odd one is out. One experienced tanguera enjoys playing with strangers who invite her formally. She: mirada. He: cabeceo. She: makes a silly face. What would you do, if you were in his shoes? She's waiting for his reaction. If he freezes, looks away, or loses his courage, then what's the point of dancing these playful Tanturi pieces with him? But if he smiles or makes a face in return — then he's clearly the one.

Mutual Care and Respect

Mutual care and respect for your partner, as well as for everyone else at the milonga, is the solid foundation on which you can build a wonderful experience. Seeing the other as equal is paramount; without this, your search for bliss will always fall short. How do you know if you're *not* seeing someone as equal? This happens whenever you consciously or unconsciously grade, compare, or judge another's *value* — when you construct mental hierarchies of participants. If your focus is on ranking yourself or your partners within such a hierarchy, you're setting yourself up for disappointment. Why? Because competition is an outward pursuit, while bliss is found in the opposite direction — bliss is inward.

The only kind of hierarchy that may be relevant in this context is the hierarchy of your own *personal experience*, which is very different from ranking your *perceived value of other people*. Your experiences dancing with various partners naturally fall along your personal pain-pleasure scale, influencing your decisions about whom to invite in the future, what kind of music to dance with them, and so on. But your *respect* for another person should not depend on your personal experiences of dancing or interacting with them.

Respect isn't a weighted scale — it's either there, or it's not. You can't have 96% of respect for your dinner date and 13% of respect for the waiter who got your order wrong. When you combine this idea with the understanding that, in our essence, we are all one, a remarkable conclusion emerges: you either respect everyone, or no one at all — not even yourself.

To foster genuine care and respect for others, you must first know who *you* are. You need to be firmly rooted in your own self-worth to recognize this same divinity in another. And once you see it in others, you begin to see this divine nature in everyone, without exception.

Kindness

When you return to the understanding that the world is a metaphorical mirror, you see why kindness is always the best choice. First and foremost, be kind to yourself, because without this you can't truly be kind to anyone else. Being kind to yourself isn't selfish — it's a necessary foundation on which you can build all your external relationships. Don't criticize or blame yourself, don't set impossible expectations, and don't bully yourself — you wouldn't allow anyone else to treat you that way, would you? In other words, don't become your own enemy. Be kind to yourself, and be kind to your body. Treat your body as you would treat a child, with his needs at the forefront.

Be kind to your partner. Your attitude toward your partner creates the environment in which you co-create your dance. You may believe you understand what's happening in your partner's inner world, but the truth of the matter is that you don't. Each one of us is unique. On top of that, even if you're dancing with the same partner, your experience creates a brand new person in your arms every time you dance. Every moment. You don't know what kind of day your partner has had or what they are experiencing right now. The best thing you can offer to another is kindness.

If you decline a verbal invitation to dance, do it with kindness. Appreciate that they chose you and had the courage to invite you. There's no need to be unkind, even if they're breaking the códigos — whatever their reason may be. Forgive right away, without hesitation. When you say "no, thank you," feel at least a bit of regret for turning them down. It will come across, and the whole encounter will feel lighter for both of you.

Kindness is the most powerful catalyst for resolving any kind of interpersonal conflict, big or small. It is the one approach that, when truly embodied, leaves no regrets. If you have to choose between being kind, being right, or being just — choose kindness. When you center in your heart and act only in alignment with the truth of who you are, your actions will naturally be kind.

How do you embody kindness? Through gratitude. Be grateful for all that is going well in your life — count your blessings. Gratitude quickly brings you back to your center, where kindness is found.

Embrace

There are several key distinctions between tango and other partner dances, and the embrace is definitely at the top of this list. The embrace defines our connection in tango; rather than focusing on moves, tango embrace invites us to focus first on *being* together, and only then on *moving* together. If I had to describe tango to someone unfamiliar with it, I would say that it's "dancing while hugging." Both dancing and hugging stimulate the release of happiness hormones, which makes it easy to see how social tango can lead to euphoria.

Intention

Outside of tango — or at least in our pre-tango life — we embrace differently. Are you holding your drinking buddy as you stumble home from a night out? Are you hugging him like he's going off to war and you may never see him again? Is it his birthday? Are you hugging your grandmother, your friend, or your lover? Is it a greeting, or a hug meant to console? Context shapes the qualities of your embrace in various ways.

In social tango, however, the qualities of our embrace depend less on context and more on intention. What do you want your embrace to convey? Do you want your embrace to look good? Do you want your embrace to feel comfortable? Do you want your embrace to communicate your emotional state to your partner? The dynamic nature of tango, together with the "medium" function of the embrace, creates something remarkable — your very intention is communicated to your partner through the embrace.

There are probably as many intentions in an embrace as there are people dancing tango. Some embraces feel as if your partner is trying to keep you from escaping. Other embraces — just the opposite — convey such a sense of freedom and independence that you sometimes have to check and make sure that your partner is still there. Of course, these are extremes, and the euphoria you're after is not in either of these directions.

You and your partner are together, willingly, to co-create magic. For that to happen, you have to orient your intention accordingly. Openness, sincerity, presence, care, readiness to communicate, to explore new depths of connection, to create and share something new and beautiful — all of these intentions ultimately aim at the same destination: bliss.

Qualities

The desired qualities of the tango embrace may be a matter of debate, however, we can simply focus on what makes sense. Beyond avoiding extremes — such as tensing your muscles or being so light that you become "transparent" or "invisible" to your partner — you generally want your embrace to feel good. It should be comfortable for both you and your partner. If you don't move past this first level of basic comfort, the higher levels of enjoyment and euphoria will remain out of reach.

Is your embrace light as a feather, or heavy like a weighted blanket? Is it elastic or rigid? Solid and reliable, or soft like a pillow? More importantly, can you *vary* these qualities? The music playing, the emotions you're feeling, and what you want to communicate to your partner can all call for different qualities in your embrace.

Generally speaking, your embrace should be oriented toward and focused on your partner. Without your partner, the embrace ceases to exist, so it only makes sense that it be about them. I vividly remember a moment from a private lesson in Buenos Aires. After I had performed the exercise correctly, the teacher suggested we dance briefly so I could absorb and anchor the information. As a reward, she said, "Now I will give you my best embrace, so this point stays with you." It surely did. As a teacher, it makes sense for her to be selective about when and how she gives it her all. But in social situations, it's a good idea to offer your best embrace to your partner every time you dance. Don't hold back — you have nothing to lose. Bliss may be waiting for you in the most unexpected moments. And adopting this attitude is one of the best ways to prime yourself to begin experiencing euphoria consistently.

Visualizations and Comparisons

Embrace your partner with your wings. Imagine that you have big angel wings extending from your shoulder blades, each wing being as tall as you are. When you embrace your partner, imagine that you're wrapping them with your wings. Each wing wraps around your partner, and both wings overlap behind their back. This exercise expands and rounds your back, which is exactly what you want — to create space and volume in your embrace while gently establishing its boundaries.

Wine in a wine glass. Picture the leader's right arm as the wall of a wine glass, while the follower's torso is the wine inside. The leader creates the boundary of the embrace while also giving the follower freedom to move within it. The leader's arm is not fixed in one spot on the follower's back. This allows the embrace to "breathe" — to gently open and close as both partners choose. The goal is to make your embrace both fluid and structured at the same time.

Closeness and Sexuality

When I was describing the captivating qualities of tango to a non-tanguera friend, she asked, "Don't you sometimes get so wound-up while dancing that you get turned on?"

It's a fair question. From the outside, all the reasons seem to be there: the lights are dimmed, there is a beautiful woman in my arms embracing me sensually, and music, bursting with passion, is adding fuel to the fire and stirring up emotions. But in order for a man to get aroused, his thoughts have to be oriented in the direction of sex. Libido is, first and foremost, a psychological phenomenon, and only then a physiological one.

What's the difference between tango and lust? The difference is in the direction of your *thoughts* while dancing. If your mind is occupied with thoughts of foreplay and sex, your energy will reflect this, and your dance will feel like little more than a disguise. Dance or lust is like looking her in the eyes or staring at her chest. One is a dialogue between souls; the other, a primal desire to possess flesh.

During my tango childhood, while visiting an unfamiliar city, I once accidentally joined an intermediate class. Up to that point, all my lessons had been in open embrace, but this time was different. "Now we're going to do this in close embrace!" — the teacher's words sent a chill up my spine. To make matters worse, I got paired with a beautiful Brazilian girl with curly hair and soft skin. On the surface, I tried to keep my composure; inside, I was panicking. "Ok, here we go." I quickly had to come to terms with being close to a beautiful stranger while remaining cool. Without fully realizing it, I was afraid that I would get aroused.

I didn't. That experience, along with others that followed, made it clear to me that arousal is a direct consequence of the content of my thoughts — and that is something I can control. In every moment, I have a choice. I can decide what to think about and which way to direct my mind. Whether or not I become sexually aroused is entirely up to me.

It's a well-known fact that it's impossible to *not* think of something specific. The classic "don't think of a pink elephant" example comes to mind — the image is evoked instantly, no matter what. Our subconscious doesn't understand negative commands, so the very thing we try to avoid is often what surfaces, simply because that's where our energy is directed. The solution is not to suppress these thoughts, but to replace them with what we *want* to focus on. In our case, it's simple: place your full attention on the dance.

Of course, tango or lust isn't simply "black or white." There's a gray area, and it helps to understand the factors at play and recognize what's really happening. In simple terms, you don't want to mistake what's often called a "tango crush" for being in love. Closeness, hugs, and physical touch release oxytocin, which can make you feel like you're falling in love. A common mistake among tango beginners is jumping to conclusions about the other person's emotions and assuming they feel the same way.

There will be times when the bliss you and your partner feel is real, the physical and chemical reactions are real, but the emotions of love and romance that may surface during a tanda aren't necessarily mutual. The truth is that there are two people dancing, each with their own character, desires, and plans for the next day. More often than not, it's just a tango crush. Such is the bittersweet nature of tango.

Try not to get attached to a specific partner, no matter how wonderful it feels to dance with them. You can experience bliss dancing with many people. The best thing you can do is not limit yourself.

The 3 Types of Embrace

Some tango dancers have certain psychological barriers when it comes to the embrace. They may feel that a close embrace is too much for them — too intimate, too vulnerable, or even too painful — and they prefer to dance in an open embrace. There's absolutely nothing wrong with that choice — there's no right or wrong way to embrace. However, this small detail can sometimes become a subtle barrier to bliss. *When it's always there,* that seemingly short distance of the open embrace can make it harder to reach the state of euphoria you're seeking.

How can fifteen centimeters between us be a barrier to bliss? I see bliss as a process of unification — a feeling of merging into oneness with everything. We'll explore this idea in more depth in the next chapter, but for now, it's enough to imagine that the essence of bliss lies in this process of merging. A close embrace naturally creates this opportunity: your and your partner's upper bodies melt together until it's hard to tell where one ends and the other begins.

An open embrace definitely allows for perfect connection, communication, and intimacy. Certain qualities of your embrace — like elasticity and movement dynamics — can lead to euphoria, making both of you feel like you're flying together. Still, compared with its close counterpart, open embrace renders the two of you as separate entities. You can both be on the same wave, however, there are clearly two separate people riding it. Also, close embrace tends to communicate trust and acceptance almost instantly.

I personally prefer the idea of a *breathing* embrace — one that naturally opens and closes depending on what each moment calls for. Sometimes the dynamics of the musical composition invite an open embrace to allow for more expansive or complex figures; other times, a close embrace is exactly what's needed to share a subtle but intense emotion together. You want your embrace to be alive — to breathe, to adapt when necessary. You want your embrace to adjust to the emotional component of the music. A breathing embrace gives both partners more freedom and the opportunity to continually renegotiate their embrace, rather than maintaining a fixed structure.

Consider this opening and closing as a metaphor for "going away" and "reuniting" with your partner. The moments of reunion — the closing of the embrace — can feel even sweeter than if you had danced the entire composition in close embrace. On my personal scale of enjoyment, in terms of proximity to bliss, the strictly open embrace comes third, the close embrace second, and the breathing embrace comes first.

Focus

The early years of your tango journey require that you focus on your posture, stability, technique, steps, and figures. As you practice and internalize these elements, they become second nature and require less of your conscious attention. Over time, the basics slowly fade into the background of your awareness. If bliss is your goal, you want to devote most of your attention to your embrace.

Wait — what about the music? Doesn't it deserve just as much of your attention as your partner? I would say no. The music, though a brilliant expression of genius and love, is both ethereal and fleeting — there's nothing there. Your partner, on the other hand, is a living, breathing human being in your arms. The music, no matter how full of emotion, cannot *feel* anything, while your partner senses what's happening inside you with surprising sensitivity. Holding another human being is not something to take for granted; the music will always be there. Most of your attention should be focused on your partner, which essentially means focusing on your embrace.

> **INVERTED EMBRACE EXERCISE**
>
> Dance one composition in an inverted embrace — as if you and your partner have switched roles, but without actually changing them. It's not a trivial exercise, so don't be discouraged if it doesn't work right away. Focus less on the figures, which will probably feel challenging, and more on the sensations within this unfamiliar embrace. What feels different? What feels comfortable? How does your arm handle its new responsibilities?

Another thing to keep in mind is that the feeling of your embrace is what stays with your partner long after the tanda is finished. If your embrace is exceptional, that wonderful sensation can stay with your partners indefinitely, and they will seek out opportunities to dance with you again and again. Your musicality, creativity, emotional expression, and floor craft all matter and should not be overlooked. Still, the way you embrace is how your partners remember you.

The Hand Embrace

The tango embrace is definitely on the list of all things fractal. Within it lies what some dancers call the "second embrace" — the way we hold our partner's hand. The way your fingers wrap around your partner's hand mirrors the embrace itself. Over the years, I've come to appreciate how important are the qualities of this hand connection: palm to palm, all fingers gently wrapped around the partner's hand, held at a comfortable height, with a comfortable angle and tone. Each of these details plays a vital role in creating a proper connection.

> **NO HAND EMBRACE EXERCISE**
>
> Dance one composition without the hand embrace. Instead, put your free hand on your partner's shoulder. Begin in a close embrace, then switch to an open embrace for a while before returning to close embrace. Reintroduce the hand embrace, then release it again. Notice what happens in your free arm and hand as a result of these transitions. Pay particular attention to any habits you may have developed — gripping too tightly, lacking tone, pushing, pulling, or holding your partner's thumb — and gently correct them. Each time you return to the hand embrace, focus your attention fully on your partner's hand. "Embrace" it slowly, using the same care and qualities as in your primary embrace.

The Back Connection

An astounding amount of information can be perceived through a proper connection between your hand and your partner's back. Especially when your partner fully engages their spirals, you can sense everything about where they are and where they're going — simply through this point of contact. This happens because all our muscle groups are linked by what are known as "fascia trains[54]" — connective tissues that run throughout the body. An engaged or disengaged, expanded or contracted spiral can be clearly perceived through your hand on your partner's back.

The key to a good back connection lies in the amount of pressure each partner applies to the other's back. More precisely, it's about balance — the pressure should be evenly shared between partners, 50-50. One of my teachers once described it beautifully: "Fill your partner's hand with your back." In other words, give some of your upper-body mass — not weight — to your partner.

During my tango adolescence, several teachers told me, "Don't hold me — I'll hold on to you." That advice shifted my focus toward finding the "sweet spot" in the middle. Rounding your back slightly and embodying the volume of your embrace helps you offer your back to your partner. Beyond being a rich channel of information, the back connection is also an essential element that preserves the structural integrity of your couple's embrace during dynamic turns and figures.

---

[54] Myers, T.W. Anatomy Trains: Myofascial Meridians for Manual Therapists and Movement Professionals. Churchill Livingstone, 2001.

Communication

"No matter what happens, don't say 'sorry,'" my partner tells me, looking into my eyes a minute before our first performance. She's right — miscommunications happen, but speaking during a performance isn't comme il faut.

You accidentally step on her toes. You miss her slowing down and throw her off axis. You miscommunicate. What do you do? The first reflex is to say, "I'm sorry." But saying *anything* — even "sorry" — especially in the middle of a beautiful tanda, just doesn't feel right. So what can you do instead? A good friend and a wonderful tanguera once taught me a simple, elegant solution without saying a word: instead of saying "sorry," she gently squeezed my hand.

Pure and simple. The beauty of it goes even further — rather than replying with "don't worry about it," you gently squeeze back. Genius.

Many followers would agree that dancing with their eyes closed feels wonderful. With less unnecessary information coming in, it's easier to fully immerse yourself in the music and the tactile sensations of the dance. But in a crowded or chaotic ronda, an extra pair of eyes can prevent serious accidents. What do you do when your partner is unknowingly leading you on a collision course with another couple? You ground yourself and press your left hand into his back to communicate: "stop." And just like in the earlier example, an appreciative partner can respond with a gentle squeeze of the hand — a silent "thank you." This is where nonverbal communication is particularly useful — in tango códigos, saying "thank you" while dancing signals to your partner that the dance is over. So, unless that's what you mean to communicate, you shouldn't say those words during the dance. (Not that I've ever made that mistake or anything.)

> **STOPPING THE LEADER EXERCISE**
>
> Try this exercise while dancing at a práctica. When the leader is about to take a back step — whether circular or linear — the follower grounds herself and presses her left hand into the leader's back to signal "stop." Just like in the "Musical Chairs" exercise, the leader should immediately abort the back step, no matter what.

The key to these subtle forms of communication is the authenticity of your intention. It works best when you truly care about your partner and your goal in dancing with them is to make them feel even better than they did before. Nonverbal communication — and social tango in particular — unmasks everyone on the dance floor. There's no way to pretend; you can only communicate what's actually there.

It took me some time to shift from saying "sorry" to expressing it nonverbally. I still slip up occasionally, but it's nowhere near the ingrained habit it once was. Give it a try — the tango community as a whole can only benefit if we talk less and communicate more.

The Key to Softness

For most of my tango adolescence I searched for a way to soften my embrace. It turns out to be far from simple — and it has nothing to do with muscle mass or body type. It took several years, but eventually I struck gold: I discovered how to make my embrace truly gentle and comfortable. Several followers noticed the change and offered the best kind of compliment — they described my embrace as soft and cozy, like a pillow. What changed?

I began to fully stretch out my spirals. I'm again referring to the two main spirals that cross the body in the shape of an "X." In dancing, I started to dissociate more while expanding the engaged spiral — the one that runs from the standing foot to the opposite shoulder. Stretching out that spiral means sending two waves of expansion that both begin at the pelvis: one upward, through the dissociating core into the opposite shoulder, and the other downward, through the standing leg into the foot, the metatarsals, and the toes. Here, pushing the floor is essential.

What's the difference between stretching out my spirals and simple dissociation? Here's an experiment: take any malleable cylindrical object — an empty aluminum soda can, for example — and twist it. What happens to its height? Since metal doesn't easily expand, the can becomes shorter. Our bodies are far more complex and lack the perfect symmetry of a soda can, so simple dissociation affects not only your vertical level but also the orientation, position, and alignment of your upper body. In short, if you don't expand your spirals, dissociation will throw a wrench into your axis, and, by transitivity, into your embrace.

Expanding my spirals, especially during turns and circular figures, helps me maintain my upper body orientation toward my partner without compromising my level, angle, or posture. I discovered that the softness of my embrace is directly connected to how *accommodating* I am toward my partner. Stretching out my spirals allowed me to stay fully with my partner, no matter the figure or step. Once I learned how to do this, it completely transformed my tango walk as well. My obliques were sore for two days after that lesson — but it was the good kind of pain, and it was absolutely worth it.

The way you embrace is deeply connected to your psychology. Expanding your spirals is where "giving it everything you've got" truly comes into play. You want to feel your obliques lengthening, along with all the muscle groups in your expanding spiral. Explore your limits and, if it feels good, gently push them. Find delight in the sensation of stretching. Explore the full length of your spirals and notice any points of tension you might want to release. When you give it your all and avoid cutting corners, your partners will find your embrace softer, more comfortable, and far more enjoyable.

Compromise

Tango, like any partnership, requires compromise. You always want to be looking for ways to find common ground — to adjust and adapt by asking yourself, "What can I change to better accommodate my partner?" For the duration of this tanda there is a *we*, an *us*. This shared entity can thrive only when both partners are willing to compromise.

If that attitude is missing — if, for instance, you prioritize being right or insist on doing exactly what your teacher told you — the dance will quickly become a burden for your partner. Even if you're completely right, over time you may find that fewer people want to dance with you. Your *intention* is always communicated to your partner. Being right might feel satisfying for a moment, but it's nothing compared to the joy of truly riding the same wave together.

This genuine sense of "together" can only exist when you're constantly reaching out to your partner.

When you reflect on how tango actually works, you'll see that its entire essence is built on compromise. Think of what's required to take even a single step together: the leader proposes a movement, the follower feels it and begins to respond, the leader senses how and where the follower is *actually* moving, then adjusts to match. This continuous cooperation is what allows the couple to dance. Without the willingness to compromise from both partners, the entire system falls apart. Your attitude toward your partner is everything.

Modeling and Mirroring

Early in my tango journey, I discovered something profound. The movement qualities I enjoy most in my partners are the ones I want to model in my own body. In other words, I can inspire and bring out the best movement dynamics in my partner by embodying those same qualities first — by emphasizing them in my own dance. I remember how silly it felt in a group class to ask my partner to dissociate more while my own torso was as solid as a log. The phrase "lead by example" takes on a whole new meaning in tango.

Psychology tells us that we often mirror others without even realizing it, and the closer the relationship, the stronger this effect becomes. In tango, the embrace creates an incredibly close connection, so mirroring tends to be especially pronounced. What's more, in tango we don't mirror by observing — we mirror by perceiving our partner's energy directly through the embrace. Body tone, movement texture, axis dynamics, spirals — there's virtually no limit to what we can mirror in our dance. Mirroring can be an easy way to "get on the same wave" with your partner. Sometimes, finding the right partner to mirror can be your ticket to bliss.

The deeper you go into mirroring your partner, the more hidden treasures you may find. For example, you can learn an incredible amount simply by mirroring your dance partners. Of course, it may take some time, learning, and practice to reach the point when you can mirror your partners — but once you're there, it's too valuable an opportunity to pass up. You may start having epiphanies not only during private lessons or prácticas but even at milongas. Kinesthetic learning through mirroring is powerful, deep, and long-lasting because the information goes straight into your body, bypassing your other senses and the analytical mind.

Another wonderful aspect of mirroring is play. When you're tuned in to your partner's energy, there are practically no limits to how much fun you can have with it. Beyond simple reflection, you can start switching things up and doing the opposite. Below are some playful ideas you may want to explore.

Call and Response. Many tango compositions have "call and response" — sections where a musical passage played by one instrument (the call) is then echoed, answered, or contrasted by another (the response). A clear example is Francisco Canaro's *Parque Patricios*, starting around the 2:00 mark. This musical dialogue offers a perfect opportunity for a similar exchange in the dance: one partner interprets the call, the other — the response.

Intertwining Melodies. Tango music tends to be complex — each instrument has its own part. When played together, these parts layer and dovetail to form the full composition. Sometimes two instruments take the spotlight, weaving distinct melodies that play and dance around each other. In compositions with vocals, this dynamic often appears between the singer's melody and the instrumental line. In dance, turns can mirror this relationship beautifully. The partner on the inside of the turn, pivoting or moving along a smaller radius, naturally takes the slower, sparser part — like the vocal line — while the partner on the outside, covering more ground, tends to take the denser melody of the instruments.

Asymmetry. Most movements in tango are symmetrical — the couple often moves as one entity. The experience of symmetry is deeply satisfying on its own, but there's more to explore if you're willing to push the boundaries. Asymmetry happens when partners move in opposite ways — for instance, when each steps to their right or both go back. This requires a certain amount of coordination from the leader, who must lead one movement while making another, but the challenge is well worth it.

COORDINATION EXERCISE

You can do this exercise alone. Set a metronome to a slow tempo, or play a slow tango. Each beat represents one step. At any given moment, you have only three possible directions to step with your free foot: forward, to the side (the same side as the free foot), or back — just like when dancing. Now, let's turn it into a coordination exercise. Each time you step, simultaneously point your finger in a direction *other* than the one you're stepping. This pointed direction will be the direction of your *next* step. The challenge lies not only in managing the asynchrony between intention and movement, but

> also in planning ahead to make sure you won't break the "three options only" rule.

Mirroring becomes especially important when you begin exploring the Y-axis — the vertical level of your dance. This often-overlooked aspect can quite literally add a new *dimension* to your tango. But if you venture there, you and your partner must explore it together; without mirroring, it simply won't work. Mirroring is a skill you can practice, refine, and master, and I highly recommend doing so — particularly if it doesn't yet come naturally to you. Mirroring can reveal new pathways to connection, expression, and ultimately, tango bliss.

Polarity

Men and women alike have both masculine and feminine traits and facets of their personalities[55]. While our biology clearly distinguishes two sexes, there is a sliding scale between the masculine and the feminine aspects of our psyche. Depending on the situation — and ultimately as the result of our own choice — we embody these various traits and shift toward one side or the other. For most people, these shifts are subtle; we tend to stay near our personal "sweet spot," the place where we feel most at home.

---

[55] Deida, D. The Way of the Superior Man. Sounds True, 1997.

Tango roles are polarized with straightforward simplicity: leading is masculine, and following is feminine. Regardless of sex, gender, or orientation, each time you lead, you embody more of your masculine; each time you follow, you embody more of your feminine. Leading and the masculine creates space and boundaries, offers initiative, direction, and protection, proposes movement, then waits and accompanies. Following and the feminine takes her time and fills the space with beauty, adornos and embellishments — flowing, accepting, and surrendering. The masculine is structure and pattern, foundation, electromagnetism, doing, the finite. The feminine is texture and flavor, grace, content, beauty, gravity, being, the infinite.

When I first started learning tango, one of my personal goals was to become a better man. I was recently divorced and single, and I knew that my future wife will deserve nothing less than someone who would always protect and care for her. Tango helped me achieve this goal in a profound way. A leader in tango is, above all, a gentleman. I offer my hand, hold doors, and pull out chairs for women not because they are incapable — they most certainly are — but because I choose to be this way. Gallantry and chivalry are inseparable from tango, as they are built on the same principle: the masculine taking care of the feminine.

There's a story from the start of one of my favorite tango festivals that has stayed with me ever since. I had just danced a tanda with a wonderful follower friend of mine — let's call her Mary. As the next tanda began, I stood near the DJ table watching the dancers. Two people nearby were chatting. One asked, "When is Sam going to arrive? He should be here by now." Sure enough, I spotted Sam and Mary dancing together in the outer ronda, approaching us. When the first song of the tanda ended, Sam saw his friend by the DJ booth. Overjoyed to see his friend, Sam walked a couple of steps over to greet him, leaving Mary alone on the dance floor. Sam and his friend hugged and began talking while Mary stood there, visibly upset at being left mid-tanda, playfully adding a child-like pout for dramatic effect.

Meanwhile, the next composition started playing. Without thinking twice, I walked over to Mary, we embraced and started dancing as if nothing had happened. By the time Sam turned to come back, it was too late — we were already off. Of course, I wouldn't have done this if the three of us weren't good friends, but the message behind the moment is clear: the masculine shouldn't stop caring for the feminine just because a tango composition is over.

After a successful cabeceo, it's important for the leader to walk over to the follower, offer his hand, and escort the follower onto the dance floor. Likewise, when the tanda ends, it's important for the leader to offer his arm and — if she accepts his offer — accompany the follower back to her seat, or wherever she wishes to go. This isn't because the follower can't navigate on her own. These seemingly outdated traditions matter because tango is, at its core, a dance between the masculine and the feminine. Everything that happens before and after the embrace is very much part of the dance itself.

In much of Western culture, chivalry has largely fallen by the wayside, displaced by the societal movement to empower women. Don't get me wrong — I fully support women's rights and equal opportunity — but social tango offers a space where we can continue to play the game between two distinct and complementary poles: the masculine and the feminine.

Also, consider the following. Walking up to the follower after a successful cabeceo, while maintaining eye contact, and then extending your hand is the best way to avoid any confusion. What if two followers sitting next to each other were looking at you when you nodded your head? Or worse, what if another leader nearby nodded at your chosen follower? Walking out on the dance floor alone and expecting your chosen partner to come to you invites all sorts of misunderstandings.

Another important point is navigational safety, which is always the leader's responsibility. When a leader says, "Meet me on the dance floor," he's implicitly adding, "…and make sure to watch for cross-traffic," effectively shifting that responsibility to the follower. Starting a tanda this way makes it harder for the follower to relax into her feminine role and fully trust the leader to take care of her safety. It may also leave her wondering how this tanda will end — "Is he going to leave me alone in the middle of the dance floor and walk away?"

When a tanda ends, people walk in every direction at once, and the dance floor quickly becomes chaotic. One hallmark of an exceptional tanda is that the follower may feel a little disoriented afterward — sometimes bliss makes you forget your own name. Whether she was so immersed in the dance that her eyes were closed and now she isn't quite sure where she is, or the twelve minutes of follower mode altered her proprioception, she shouldn't have to navigate on her own just because the music stopped. No one wants to be jolted out of a wonderful state. A caring leader will allow the follower to bask in that feeling, never leaving her alone on the dance floor. This holds true regardless of whether the leader enjoyed the tanda or not.

A distinctive quality of the feminine is the desire for the masculine to magically know what she wants. When the tuned-in masculine makes this proposition, her "yes" isn't just "okay" — it's more like "OH GOD, YES!" Both get a rush of happiness hormones: the masculine, who thinks that the good proposition was his idea, and the feminine, who got him reading her mind. The result is pure euphoria.

When you explore these ideas deeply, you realize that the masculine and feminine roles are not written in stone. It can be a great source of fun to switch things up and play with these dynamics in the dance. Tango shows you a glimpse of an entire world of role-playing and games, where you can write your own rules — and break them if you want.

The spark, the charge, the play between the masculine and the feminine is the essence of polarity in tango. The polarization of roles is what allows us to lead and to follow, making tango possible in the first place. The masculine-feminine dynamics create the perfect conditions for both leader and follower to experience that unmistakable, lit-up-like-fireworks, joy-on-overdrive tango bliss.

Oneness

Spiritual and esoteric teachings have long expressed what today's science is beginning to confirm — that, at the deepest level, everything is one. We don't need to dive into the mechanics of this idea or contemplate the philosophy behind it; instead, we can explore its experiential dimension in the context of social tango.

How does oneness feel in the embrace? What can we do to experience it? We can consider several stages of moving from polarity — or duality, if you prefer — toward oneness. Each stage brings you closer to that sense of unity, and closer to experiencing pure euphoria on the dance floor.

Riding the Wave Together

The feeling of riding the same tango wave with your partner can be sublime. But how does it actually work? The idea that the human body is a bio-antenna offers some insight. Tango music, combined with the physical connection of the embrace, creates the perfect conditions for two people to tune into the same frequency for extended periods of time. All it takes is a gentle surrender, a willingness to give up a part of your cognitive control to the music.

Normally, when we're awake and conscious, we direct and control our muscles, and our movements. There's usually a purpose behind our every action, and our movements serve that purpose. Whether with full awareness or on "autopilot," we are the ones who initiate our movements. The mind focuses on an intention, the brain converts that thought into electrical impulses, and those impulses activate the muscle groups, producing motion. When we're on autopilot, we delegate a part of our control to our *muscle memory*, while our minds are occupied by something else.

Tango offers a completely different context — there's no specific purpose behind our movements. When we dance and ride the wave of tango music, we hand over part of our cognitive control to the music itself. We stop initiating our movements and shift from being the "initiator" to being the "observer," a supervisor who maintains executive say, but mostly oversees the process. The music *dances us.*

The beauty of having two partners in the embrace is that the one already on the wave can help bring the other onto it. This likely happens more often than we realize, since some people find it easier to catch the wave than others. If you ever find this process challenging or elusive, don't worry — sometimes all it takes is tuning in to your partner with the clear intention of joining them on the wave. When that becomes your focus, there's a good chance they'll take you there.

Riding the wave alone can bring tremendous joy — just ask fine artists and surfers. But riding it together with your tango partner adds another dimension to your experience. It's not just about riding the same emotional rollercoaster together; after all, watching a movie with your friend can give you that opportunity. The difference is that the wave of tango music, combined with the alchemy of the embrace, carries both dancers in the direction of *merging*. Merging with the music, with each other, with all of existence — after a while, it no longer matters exactly what is being merged. Riding the wave of tango music together with your partner takes you to bliss.

Moving as One

When both partners set out with the shared goal of attuning to one another — of connecting deeply on all possible levels — something extraordinary begins to happen. Leading and following — the masculine and feminine polarity — give way to something deeper: the energies of two individuals start to merge. Over time, this merging brings about a remarkable transformation — you and your partner begin to move as one. Your movements are no longer led and followed; they're not even synchronized in the traditional sense. Your movements and those of your partner become the *same movements*. Both of you move from a single impulse — a shared signal coming through the merged bio-antenna of your bodies.

In that moment, the couple becomes the *Four-Legged Tango Machine — la Máquina Tanguera*. You are no longer two separate people; you're effectively sharing the same nervous system, the same mind that now spans across both of your bodies. This merging, this becoming one with your partner, is the purest essence of bliss in tango.

Dissolving Space and Time

"Your lowest point is the doorway to your highest self. For when the heart breaks, something far deeper is taking place than mere misfortune. We often don't realize the value of the darkness until it has passed, for only in the absence of light that we learn to become the light. The human mind seeks comfort, but the soul stirs for change. It longs to grow, not to stay the same. The meaning of life is just to be alive. And yet, we resist the very currents that are pulling us into deeper awareness of that aliveness. You're not here to chase happiness like a dog chasing its tail — happiness is a byproduct of becoming whole, and wholeness requires contrast: dark and light, sorrow and joy, breaking and rebuilding. So when it hurts — let it hurt. Don't run — sit with it. Listen to it. And when you finally rise from

it, you'll realize the joy was never in the outcome, but in the transformation. Feed the soul, not the ego. Choose evolution over escape, and the life you're searching for will no longer be something you find — it will be something you are."
—Alan Watts

Tango bliss is a kind of trance. You're fully present — here and now — yet you're in an altered state of consciousness. Your sense of time begins to shift: at first, time slows down, then it stops, and eventually disappears altogether. You don't just lose track of time — you become unaware that time even exists. Your perception of space, of objects, of people, and even of your own body begins to change. Everything is still there, yet it all seems to dissolve into an ever-expanding sense of merging.

After a while, you can no longer tell where your body ends and your partner's body begins. But the merging doesn't stop there — you merge with the music, with the space, and with everyone around you. You merge with the ronda, becoming a massive, counterclockwise vortex of energy. You merge with the planet and the solar system, with the galaxy, and with the entire universe, until all you feel is Oneness. Your persona, along with all its thoughts and concerns, fades into irrelevance. The world is still there, but there is no one there to perceive it. The observer and the observed have become one — turning into walking-on-whipped-cream-clouds, weightless, sparkling bliss.

If you enjoyed this book, and would like to help me translate it into your native language to make it accessible to more people, please contact me at info@blissfultango.com

A Very Special Thank You

Adeline Ireland
Alla Drugova
Amelie Leipprand
Anastasia Martini
Anya Kovalieva
Balázs Gyenis
Candela Ramos
Csilla Grandi
Daniel Willmott
Derek Tang
Dimitris Bronowski
Elena Frishman
Elena Jovanoska
Elena Sergienko
Emilia Kumpulainen
György Horváth
Hagen Schröter
Ilona Glinarsky
Iris Rogozhyna
Irina Pistoletova
Jade Ng
János Bicsár
John Gerencser
Juan Alba
Ksenia Deresh

Malachai Payne
Maria Moreno
Maria Shagieva
Mariana Soler
Márk Cseh
Mary Li
Mia Machač-Tóth
Miles Tangos
Olga Valeyka
Petar Pavlov
Polina Fadeyeva
Raúl Palladino
Rebeka Bangó
Robert Le
Semeon Kukormin
Sergiy Podbolotnyi
Silvana Anfossi
Simon Kozma
Tabea Bley
Tabea Schwirblat
Tatiana Yuldasheva
Tekla Gogrichiani
Thomas Rieser
Timea Zékány
Veronica Toumanova

blissfultango.com

Recommendations

tangofulness.com

"Tangofulness: Exploring connection, awareness, and meaning in tango" is a soulful exploration of Argentine tango as a philosophy of life, a dance of awareness, connection, and presence that transcends movement to become a meditation on being. Available in 14 languages.

thecurioustanguero.com/hugandletgo

"Hug and Let Go: Poems of Argentine Tango" captures the poetry of the tango embrace: fleeting, tender, and eternal. Through vivid, lyrical verses, it weaves stories of longing, loss, and the delicate art of surrender. Available in English, Spanish, Italian and German.

verotango.com/books

"Why Tango: More essays on learning, dancing and living tango argentino" Whether you are a total beginner or an experienced dancer, in Veronica's essays you will discover a rich source of knowledge and inspiration as she tackles complex psychological, social and pedagogical issues in tango as a social dance and a performing art. Her essays offer a profound and well-articulated reflection on the contemporary tango scene, supported by insights from psychology, neuroscience, biomechanics and bodymind techniques. Available in 16 languages.

www.ingramcontent.com/pod-product-compliance
Lightning Source LLC
Chambersburg PA
CBHW051126160426
43195CB00014B/2362